D1302725

A CALL
TO
AMERICA

★★★★★

**Other Random House Value Publishing
titles of interest:**

The Complete Book of U.S. Presidents

The Inaugural Addresses of the Presidents

A Pictorial History of the U.S. Presidents

Words from Our Presidents

The Wit & Wisdom of Abraham Lincoln

The Wit & Wisdom of Harry Truman

★★★★★

A CALL
TO
AMERICA

INSPIRING QUOTATIONS FROM
THE PRESIDENTS OF THE UNITED STATES

EDITED BY BRYAN CURTIS

GRAMERCY BOOKS
NEW YORK

This 2004 edition is published by Gramercy Books,
an imprint of Random House Value Publishing,
a division of Random House, Inc., New York,
by arrangement with Rutledge Hill Press.

Gramercy is a registered trademark
and the colophon is a trademark of Random House, Inc.

Random House
New York • Toronto • London • Sydney • Auckland
www.randomhouse.com

Design by Gore Studio Inc.

Printed and bound in the United States

A catalog record for this title is available from
the Library of Congress.

ISBN 0-517-22323-6

10 9 8 7 6 5 4 3 2 1

I have been very lucky
to have two men with very different views on
the political process play an important role in my life.
This book is dedicated to them.

In memory of my father, Ralph Curtis

I never once heard my father say whom he voted for—
and it's not as if I never asked. I have no clue whether he was a
Democrat or a Republican. Yet, never did I hear him offer a prayer
in church when he did not pray for our leaders.
It didn't matter to him what political party they belonged to.

For my stepfather, Bill Caldwell

My stepfather is probably the most passionately political man
I know. I greatly admire his strong feelings about what is right
and which party is right.

CONTENTS

CONTENTS

PREFACE

FROM THE HUMBLE yet heroic beginnings of the United States, we as citizens have looked to our presidents for leadership, encouragement, and comfort. George Washington rallied the citizens of a new country when he said, "Let us therefore animate and encourage each other, and show the world that a free man, contending for his liberty of his own ground, is superior to any slavish mercenary on earth." Almost a hundred years later, Abraham Lincoln called out for Americans to mend their broken nation, declaring, "In all our rejoicings, let us neither express nor cherish any hard feelings toward any citizen who, by his vote, has differed with us. Let us at all times remember that all American citizens are brothers of common country, and should do well together in the bonds of fraternal feeling."

Throughout our history, our presidents have inspired us to rise to the unique challenges of each era. Franklin Roosevelt used the following words to encourage Americans during World War II: "Sacrifices that we and our allies are making impose upon us all a sacred obligation to see to it that out of this war we and our children will gain something better than mere survival." As our nation focused on civil rights in the 1960s, Lyndon Johnson challenged each citizen of this country to look beyond personal prejudice when he said, "Until justice is blind to color, until education is unaware of race, until opportunity is unconcerned with the color of men's skins, emancipation will be a proclamation but not a fact." And, most recently, George W. Bush comforted and inspired America after the terrorist attacks on September 11, 2001, when he proclaimed, "Today our nation saw evil, the very worst of human nature. And we responded with the best of America."

These are just a few examples of times when America looked to its chief executive for leadership, for inspiration, and for comfort. In this book you will find more than 1,500 additional quotations from our presidents that have touched a life, healed a nation, and inspired people to be their very best.

GEORGE WASHINGTON

1ST PRESIDENT • 1789–1797
Born: February 22, 1732, in Westmoreland County, Virginia
Died: December 17, 1799, in Mt. Vernon, Virginia

Wife: Martha Dandridge Custis

Religion: Episcopalian

Education: No formal education

Other political offices: Member of Continental Congress

Although this man who came to be known as the father of our country had only a grammar school education, George Washington ranks as one of the most influential and respected presidents in our history. With his ability to inspire confidence in his troops and unite a new nation, Washington almost single-handedly created a new government. Although his popularity could have allowed him to remain in office as long as he desired, he chose to leave after two terms.

I hope I shall always possess firmness and virtue enough to maintain what I consider the most enviable of all titles, the character of an honest man.

*

Let us therefore animate and encourage each other, and show the world that a free man, contending for his liberty on his own ground, is superior to any slavish mercenary on earth.

*

There is nothing which can better deserve our patronage than the promotion of science and literature. Knowledge is in every country the surest basis of public happiness.

*

Ninety-nine percent of the failures come from people who have the habit of making excuses.

*

It is our duty to make the best of our misfortunes, and not to suffer passion to interfere with our interest and public good.

*

Few men have virtue to withstand the highest bidder.

*

Associate yourself with men of good quality if you esteem your own reputation, for 'tis better to be alone than in bad company.

We ought not to look back unless it is to derive useful lessons from past errors, and for the purpose of profiting by dear-bought experience.

There is no restraining men's tongues or pens when charged with a little vanity.

Be courteous to all, but intimate with few, and let those few be well tried before you give them your confidence.

To be prepared for war is one of the most effectual means of preserving peace.

I conceive that a knowledge of books is the basis on which all other knowledge rests.

Labor to keep alive in your breast that little spark of celestial fire called conscience.

My first wish is to see this plague of mankind, war, banished from earth.

It will be found an unjust and unwise jealousy to deprive a man of his natural liberty upon the supposition he may abuse it.

Precedents are dangerous things; let the reins of government then be braced and held with a steady hand, and every violation of the Constitution be reprehended: If defective let it be amended, but not suffered to be trampled upon whilst it has an existence.

To err is nature, to rectify error is glory.

I walk on untrodden ground. There is scarcely any part of my conduct which may not hereafter be drawn into precedent.

As the sword was the last resort for the preservation of our liberties, so it ought to be the first to be laid aside when those liberties are firmly established.

Let us raise a standard to which the wise and honest can repair, the rest is in the hands of God.

Discipline is the soul of an army. It makes small numbers formidable, procures success to the weak, and esteem to all.

A slender acquaintance with the world must convince every man that actions, not words, are the true criterion of the attachment of friends.

Happiness depends more upon the internal frame of a person's own mind, than on the externals in the world.

I do not enter into agreements, but with an intention of fulfilling them, and I expect the same punctuality on the part of those with whom they are made.

I have seen so many instances of the rascality of mankind, that I am convinced that the only way to make them honest, is to prevent their being otherwise.

Though, in reviewing the incidents of my administration, I am unconscious of intentional error, I am, nevertheless, too sensible of my defects not to think it probable that I may have committed many errors.

As Mankind becomes more liberal, they will be more apt to allow that all those who conduct themselves as worthy members of the community are equally entitled to the protections of civil government. I hope ever to see America among the foremost nations of justice and liberality.

The time is now and near at hand which must probably determine whether Americans are to be freemen or slaves; whether they are to have property they can call their own; whether their houses and farms are to be pillaged and destroyed, and themselves consigned to a state of wretchedness from which no human efforts will deliver them. The fate of unborn millions will now depend, under God, on the courage and conduct of this army. Our cruel and unrelenting enemy leaves us no choice but a brave resistance, or the most abject submission. . . . We have, therefore, to resolve to conquer or to die.

The welfare of our country is the great object to which our cares and efforts ought to be directed—And I shall derive great satisfaction from cooperation with you, in the pleasing though arduous task of ensuring to our fellow citizens the blessings which they have a right to expect from a free and equal government.

A free people ought not only to be armed but disciplined; to which end a uniform and well-digested plan is requisite.

I cannot forbear intimating to you the expediency of giving effectual encouragement as well to the introduction of new and useful inventions from abroad, as to the exertions of skill and genius in producing them at home; and of facilitating the intercourse between the distant parts of the country by a due attention to the Post Office and Post Roads.

Observe good faith and justice toward all nations. Cultivate peace and harmony with all.

Reason, too late perhaps, may convince you of the folly in misspending time.

My mother was the most beautiful woman I ever saw. All I am I owe to my mother. I attribute all my success in life to the moral, intellectual and physical education I received from her.

True friendship is a plant of slow growth, and must undergo and withstand the shocks of adversity, before it is entitled to the appellation.

Lenience will operate with greater force, in some instances than rigor. It is therefore my first wish to have all of my conduct distinguished by it.

The propitious smiles of heaven can never be expected on a nation that disregards the eternal rules of order and right which heaven itself has ordained.

Happily the Government of the United States, which gives to bigotry no sanction, to persecution no assistance, requires only that they who live under its protection should demean themselves as good citizens in giving on all occasions their effectual support.

*

The basis of our political systems is the right of the people to make and to alter their constitutions of government.

*

In proportion as the structure of a government gives force to public opinion, it is essential that public opinion should be enlightened.

Liberty, when it begins to take root, is a plant of rapid growth.

Let your heart feel for the affliction and distress of everyone.

*

The consideration that human happiness and moral duty are inseparably connected will always continue to prompt me to promote the former by inculcating the practice of the latter.

Arbitrary power is most easily established on the ruins of liberty abused to licentiousness.

The marvel of all history is the patience with which men and women submit to burdens unnecessarily laid upon them by their governments.

My observation is that whenever one person is found adequate to the discharge of a duty . . . it is worse executed by two persons, and scarcely done at all if three or more are employed therein.

Let your discourse with men of business be short and comprehensive.

The name of American, which belongs to you, in your national capacity, must always exalt the just pride of Patriotism, more than any appellation derived from local discriminations. With slight shades of difference, you have the same religion, manners, habits, and political principles. You have in a common cause fought and triumphed together, the Independence and Liberty you possess are the work of joint counsels, and joint efforts, of common dangers, sufferings, and successes.

A government is like fire, a handy servant, but a dangerous master.

JOHN ADAMS

2ND PRESIDENT • 1797–1801

Born: October 30, 1735, in Braintree, Massachusetts
Died: July 4, 1826, in Braintree, Massachusetts

Wife: Abigail Smith

Religion: Unitarian

Education: Harvard College

Other political offices: Member of Continental Congress, Member of Massachusetts State Legislature, U. S. Minister to Britain, Vice President

A signer of the Declaration of Independence, John Adams served as vice president to George Washington for eight years before being elected president. Adams devoted his life to politics, playing a lead role in the first revolutionary actions in both Boston and Philadelphia. Narrowly defeating Thomas Jefferson, Adams sought political harmony by calling upon the people to end partisan politics. Known as an intelligent and courageous statesman, Adams upheld the authority of the presidency in resisting demands for war with France over harassment of U.S. ships. Adams was the father of the sixth president, John Quincy Adams.

Yesterday the greatest question was decided which was ever debated in America; and a greater perhaps never was, nor will be, decided among men. A resolution was passed without one dissenting colony, that those United Colonies are, and of right out to be, free and independent states.

You have rights antecedent to all earthly governments; rights that cannot be repealed or restrained by human laws; rights derived from the Great Legislator of the Universe.

Let me have my farm, family and goose quill, and all the honors and offices this world has to bestow may go to those who deserve them better and desire them more. I court them now.

Liberty, according to my metaphysics, is an intellectual quality; an attribute that belongs not to fate nor chance.

No man who ever held the office of President would congratulate a friend on obtaining it. He will make one man ungrateful, and a hundred men his enemies, for every office he can bestow.

Statesmen may plan and speculate for liberty, but it is religion and morality alone which can establish the principles upon which freedom can securely stand.

Property is surely a right of mankind as real as liberty.

If national pride is ever justifiable or excusable it is when it springs not from power or riches, grandeur or glory, but from conviction of national innocence, information, and benevolence.

Let the human mind loose. It must be loosed; it will be loose. Superstition and despotism cannot confine it.

Modesty is a virtue that can never thrive in public. . . . A man must be his own trumpeter. He must get his picture drawn, his statue made, and must hire all the artists in his turn, to set about the works to spread his name, make the mob stare and gape, and perpetuate his fame.

I must study politics and war that my sons may have liberty to study mathematics and philosophy. My sons ought to study mathematics and philosophy, geography, natural history, naval architecture, navigation, commerce and agriculture in order to give their children a right to study paintings, poetry, music, architecture, statuary, tapestry and porcelain.

Society's demands for moral authority and character increase as the importance of the position increases.

The second day of July, 1776, will be the most memorable epoch in the history of America. I am apt to believe that it will be celebrated by succeeding generations as the great anniversary festival. It ought to be commemorated as the day of deliverance, by solemn acts of devotion to God Almighty. It ought to be solemnized with pomp and parade, with shows, games, sports, guns, bells, bonfires, and illuminations, from one end of this continent to the other, from this time forward for ever more.

I pray Heaven to bestow the best of blessings on this house and all that shall hereafter inhabit it. May none but honest and wise men ever rule under this roof.

The body politic is . . . a social compact, by which the whole people covenants with each citizen, and each citizen with the whole people, that all shall be governed by certain laws for the common good.

Facts are stubborn things; and whatever may be our wishes, our inclinations, or the dictates of our passions, they cannot alter the state of facts and evidence.

The only maxim of a free government ought to be to trust no man living with power to endanger the public liberty.

Old minds are like old horses: you must exercise them if you wish to keep them in working order.

Liberty cannot be preserved without a general knowledge among the people.

Think of your forefathers! Think of your posterity.

The essence of a free government consists in an effectual control of rivalries.

When people talk of the freedom of writing, speaking or thinking I cannot choose but laugh. No such thing ever existed. No such thing now exists; but I hope it will exist. But it must be hundreds of years after you and I shall write and speak no more.

A desire to be observed, considered, esteemed, praised, beloved, and admired by his fellows is one of the earliest as well as the keenest dispositions discovered in the heart of man.

We should begin by setting conscience free. When all men of all religions . . . shall enjoy equal liberty, property, and an equal chance for honors and power . . . we may expect that improvements will be made in the human character and the state of society.

> # Straight is the gate and narrow is the way that leads to liberty, and few nations, if any, have found it.

If it be the pleasure of Heaven that my country shall require the poor offering of my life, the victim shall be ready. . . . But while I do live, let me have a country, or at least the hope of a country, and that a free country.

In the midst of these pleasing ideas we should be unfaithful to ourselves if we should ever lose sight of the danger to our liberties if anything partial or extraneous should infect the purity of our free, fair, virtuous, and independent elections.

Grief drives men to serious reflection, sharpens the understanding and softens the heart.

This hand, to tyrants ever sworn the foe,
For freedom only deals the deadly blow;
Then sheathes in calm repose the vengeful blade,
For gentle peace in Freedom's hallowed shade.

The people have a right, an indisputable, unalienable, indefensible, divine right to that most dreaded and envied kind of knowledge—I mean of the character and conduct of their rulers.

❧

Employed in the service of my country abroad during the whole course of these transactions, I first saw the Constitution of the United States in a foreign country. Irritated by no literary altercation, animated by no public debate, heated by no party animosity, I read it with great satisfaction, as the result of good heads prompted by good hearts, as an experiment better adapted to the genius, character, situation, and relations of this nation and country than any which had ever been proposed or suggested.

❧

Genius is sorrow's child.

❧

It is weakness rather than wickedness which renders men unfit to be trusted with unlimited power.

❧

By my physical constitution, I am but an ordinary man. The times alone have destined me to fame—and even these have not been able to give me much.

❧

Public virtue cannot exist in a nation without private virtue, and public virtue is the only foundation of republics.

THOMAS JEFFERSON

3RD PRESIDENT • 1801–1809

Born: April 13, 1743, in Shadwell Plantation, Virginia
Died: July 4, 1826, in Monticello, near Charlottesville, Virginia

Wife: Martha Wales Skelton

Religion: No formal affiliation

Education: College of William and Mary

Other political offices: Minister to France, Governor of Virginia, Member of the Continental Congress, Secretary of State, Vice President

Thomas Jefferson, a native Virginian and a powerful advocate of liberty, constructed Monticello, his famous mountaintop home, on five thousand acres of land he inherited. At thirty-three, Jefferson drafted the Declaration of Independence and later the Virginia Statute for Religious Freedom. Among the major events of his two-term administration were the Louisiana Purchase and the Lewis and Clark expedition to the Pacific Ocean.

I hold it, that a little rebellion, now and then, is a good thing, and as necessary in the political world as storms in the physical.

He who permits himself to tell a lie once, finds it much easier to do it a second and third time, till at length it becomes habitual; he tells lies without attending to it, and truths without the world's believing him. This falsehood of the tongue leads to that of the heart, and in time depraves all its good dispositions.

The tree of liberty must be refreshed from time to time with the blood of patriots and tyrants. It is natural manure.

Delay is preferable to error.

An injured friend is the bitterest of foes.

I have sworn upon the altar of God, eternal hostility against every form of tyranny over the mind of man.

History, in general, only informs us what bad government is.

I cannot live without books.

I know no safe depository of the ultimate powers of society but the people themselves, and if we think them not enlightened enough to exercise their control with a wholesome discretion, the remedy is not to take it from them, but to inform their discretion by education.

Great innovations should not be forced on slender majorities.

I have never considered a difference of opinion in politics, in religion, in philosophy, as a cause for withdrawing from a friendship.

Resistance to tyrants is obedience to God.

The constitutions of most of our states (and of the United States) assert that all power is inherent in the people; that they may exercise it by themselves; that it is their right and duty to be at all times armed and that they are entitled to freedom of person, freedom of religion, freedom of property, and freedom of press.

I consider trial by jury as the only anchor yet imagined by man by which a government can be held to the principles of its Constitution.

Happiness is not being pained in body or troubled in mind.

The way to have safe government is not to trust it all to the one, but to divide it among the many, distributing to everyone exactly the functions in which he is competent. . . . To let the National Government be entrusted with the defense of the nation, and its foreign and federal relations. . . . The State Governments with the civil Rights, Laws, Police and administration of what concerns the State generally. The Counties with local concerns, and each ward direct the interests within itself. It is by dividing and subdividing these Republics from the great national one down through all its subordinations until it ends in the administration of everyman's farm by himself, by placing under everyone what his own eye may superintend, that all will be done for the best.

~

We must not let our rulers load us with perpetual debt. We must make our selection between economy and liberty or profusion and servitude.

~

Above all things I hope the education of the common people will be attended to, convinced that on their good sense we may rely with the utmost security for the preservation of a due degree of liberty.

~

The right of opinion shall suffer no invasion from me. Those who have acted well have nothing to fear, however they may have differed from me in opinion: those who have done ill, however, have nothing to hope; nor shall I fail to do justice lest it should be ascribed to that difference of opinion.

* *

It is neither wealth nor splendor, but tranquility and occupation which give happiness.

The God who gave us life gave us liberty at the same time.

இ

I have not observed men's honesty to increase with their riches.

இ

A wise and frugal government, which shall restrain men from injuring one another, shall leave them otherwise free to regulate their own pursuits of industry and improvement, and shall not take from the mouth of labor the bread it has earned. This is the sum of good government

இ

The spirit of resistance to government is so valuable on certain occasions that I wish it to be always kept alive.

இ

It is incumbent on every generation to pay its own debts as it goes. A principle which if acted on would save one-half the wars of the world.

Mischief may be done negatively as well as positively.

❧

I tolerate with the utmost latitude the right of others to differ from me in opinion without imputing to them criminality.

❧

Liberty is the collective body, what health is to every individual body. Without health no pleasure can be tasted by man; without liberty, no happiness can be enjoyed by society.

❧

Most bad government has grown out of too much government.

❧

No government ought to be without censors, and where the press is free, no one ever will.

❧

I am mortified to be told that, in the United States of America, the sale of a book can become a subject of inquiry, and of criminal inquiry too.

❧

Error of opinion may be tolerated where reason is left free to combat it.

❧

We are not afraid to follow truth wherever it may lead, nor to tolerate any error so long as reason is left free to combat it.

✦ ✦

When angry, count to ten before you speak. If very angry, a hundred.

✍

The will of the people . . . is the only legitimate foundation of any government, and to protect its free expression should be our first object.

✍

Only aim to do your duty, and mankind will give you credit when you fail.

✍

Peace, commerce, and honest friendship with all nations—entangling alliances with none.

✍

Question with boldness even the existence of God; because if there be one, He must more approve of the homage of reason, than that of blindfolded fear.

✍

Sometimes it is said that man cannot be trusted with the government himself. Can he, then be trusted with the government of others?

✍

That government is best which governs the least, because its people discipline themselves.

✍

In matters of principle, stand like a rock, in matters of taste, swim with the current.

The most valuable of all talents is that of never using two words when one will do.

❧

If the children are untaught, their ignorance and vices will in future life cost us much dearer in their consequences than it would have done in their correction by a good education.

❧

I have erred at times—no doubt I have erred; this is the law of human nature. For honest errors, however, indulgence may be hoped.

❧

Education . . . engrafts a new man on the native stock, and improves what in his nature was vicious and perverse into qualities of virtue and social worth . . . [accumulated knowledge] must advance the knowledge and well being of mankind, not infinitely, as some have said, but indefinitely, and to a term which one can fix or foresee.

❧

It is the multitude which possess force, and wisdom must yield to that.

❧

Our greatest happiness does not depend on the condition of life in which chance has placed us, but it is always the result of a good conscience, good health, occupation, and freedom in all just pursuits.

Indeed I tremble for my country when I reflect that God is just.

*

We all know too well the texture of the human mind, and the slipperiness of human reason, to consider differences of opinion otherwise than differences of form or feature. Integrity of views, more than their soundness, is the basis of esteem.

*

Timid men prefer the calm of despotism to the boisterous sea of liberty.

I would rather be exposed to the inconveniences attending too much liberty than those attending too small a degree of it.

Those who desire to give up freedom in order to gain Security will not have, nor do they deserve, either one.

*

It is much easier to avoid errors by having good information at first, than to unravel and correct them after they are committed.

Truth is certainly a branch of morality and a very important one to society.

∂≻

Every citizen should be a soldier. This was the case with the Greeks and Romans, and must be that of every free state.

∂≻

Enlighten the people generally, and tyranny and oppressions of body and mind will vanish like spirits at the dawn of day.

∂≻

The man who fears no truth has nothing to fear from lies.

∂≻

He who knows nothing is closer to the truth than he whose mind is filled with falsehoods and errors.

∂≻

Difference of opinion leads to enquiry, and enquiry to truth.

∂≻

Power is not alluring to pure minds.

∂≻

I love to see honest and honorable men at the helm, men who will not bend their politics to their purses nor pursue measures by which they may profit and then profit by their measures.

* *

The glow of one warm thought is to me worth more than money.

⚜

The happiest moments of my life have been the few which I have passed at home in the bosom of my family.

⚜

Life is of no value but as it brings us gratifications. Among the most valuable of these is rational society. It informs the mind, sweetens the temper, cheers our spirits, and promotes health.

⚜

Always take hold of things by the smooth handle.

Liberty is the great parent of science and of virtue; and a nation will be great in both in proportion as it is free.

If we are faithful to our country, if we acquiesce, with good will, in the decisions of the majority, and the nation moves in mass in the same direction, although it may not be that which every individual thinks best, we have nothing to fear from any quarter.

Peace and friendship with all mankind is our wisest policy, and I wish we may be permitted to pursue it.

※

Pride costs more than hunger, thirst and cold.

※

I have never been able to conceive how any rational being could propose happiness to himself from the exercise of power over others.

※

This should be a man's attitude: "Few things will disturb him at all; nothing will disturb him much."

※

Nothing can stop the man with the right mental attitude from achieving his goal; nothing on earth can help the man with the wrong mental attitude.

※

Truth between candid minds can never do harm.

※

Books constitute capital. A library book lasts as long as a house, for hundreds of years. It is not, then, an article of mere consumption but fairly of capital, and often in the case of professional men, setting out in life, it is their only capital.

※

Do not bite the bait of pleasure till you know there is no hook beneath it.

* *

The boisterous sea of liberty is never without a wave.

❧

I find the pain of a little censure, even when it is unfounded, is more acute than the pleasure of much praise.

❧

But friendship is precious, not only in the shade, but in the sunshine of life; and thanks to a benevolent arrangement of things, the greater part of life is sunshine.

❧

I am a great believer in luck, and I find the harder I work, the more I have of it.

❧

Freedom of religion, freedom of the press, trial by jury, habeas corpus, and a representative legislature . . . I consider as the essentials constituting free government, and . . . the organization of the executive is interesting as it may insure wisdom and integrity in the first place, but next as it may favor or endanger the reservation of these fundamentals.

❧

To inform the minds of the people, and to follow their will, is the chief duty of those placed at their head.

❧

With the same honest views, the most honest men often form different conclusions.

My chief object is to let the good sense of the nation have fair play, believing it will best take care of itself.

❧

The road to that glory which never dies is to use power for the support of the laws of our country, not for their destruction.

❧

[The] approbation of my fellow-citizens is the richest reward I can receive. I am conscious of having always intended to do what was best for them; and never, for a single moment, to have listened to any personal interest of my own.

❧

If, in the course of my life, it has been in any degree useful to the cause of humanity, the fact itself bears its full reward.

❧

It is impossible not to deplore our past follies and their present consequences, but let them at least be warnings against like follies in future.

❧

In the transaction of the business of my fellow citizens I cannot have escaped error. It is incident to our imperfect nature. But I may say with truth, my errors have been of the understanding, not of intention; and that the advancement of the rights and interests has been the constant motive of every measure.

I have not been in the habit of mysterious reserve on any subject, nor of buttoning up my opinions within my own doublet. On the contrary, while in public service especially, I thought the public entitled to frankness, and intimately to know whom they employed.

After the satisfaction of doing what is right, the greatest is that of having what we do approved by those whose opinions deserve esteem.

It is not wisdom alone but pubic confidence in that wisdom which can support an administration.

Opinion is power.

Continue to go straight forward, pursuing always that which is right, as the only clue which can lead us out of the labyrinth. Let nothing be spared of either reason or passion to preserve the public confidence entire as the only rock of our safety.

In a free country, every power is dangerous which is not bound up by general rules.

Principles being understood, their applications will be less embarrassing.

❧

I have the consolation . . . of having added nothing to my private fortune during my public service and of retiring with hands as clean as they are empty.

❧

In truth, man is not made to be trusted for life if secured against all liability to account.

❧

I think it is a duty in those entrusted with the administration of their affairs to conform themselves to the decided choice of their constituents.

❧

Truth advances and error recedes step by step only; and to do our fellow men the most good in our power, we must lead where we can, follow where we cannot, and still go with them, watching always the favorable moment for helping them to another step.

❧

He who has done his duty honestly, and according to his best skill and judgment, stands acquitted before God and man.

❧

The boys of the rising generation are to be the men of the next, and the solid guardians of the principles we deliver over to them.

Remember that we often repent of what we have said, but never, never of that which we have not.

✍

I will sacrifice everything but principle to procure harmony.

✍

Every difference of opinion is not a difference of principle.

✍

I believe we may lessen the danger of buying and selling votes by making the number of voters too great for any means of purchase.

✍

No man has a natural right to commit aggression on the equal rights of another, and this is all from which the laws ought to restrain him.

✍

That love of order and obedience to the laws, which so remarkably characterize the citizens of the United States, are sure pledges of internal tranquility; and the elective franchise, if guarded as the ark of our safety, will peaceably dissipate all combinations to subvert a Constitution, dictated by the wisdom, and resting on the will of the people.

✍

Should things go wrong at any time, the people will set them to rights by the peaceable exercise of their elective rights.

Laws made by common consent must not be trampled on by individuals.

Bear in mind this sacred principle, that though the will of the majority is in all cases to prevail, that will, to be rightful, must be reasonable; that the minority possess their equal rights, which equal laws must protect, and to violate would be oppression.

It is an encouraging observation that no good measure was ever proposed which, if duly pursued, failed to prevail in the end.

Man, once surrendering his reason, has no remaining guard against absurdities the most monstrous, and like a ship without a rudder, is the sport of every wind. With such persons, gullibility, which they call faith, takes the helm from the hand of reason, and the mind becomes weak.

Bear always in mind that a nation ceases to be republican only when the will of the majority ceases to be the law.

If virtuous, the government need not fear the fair operation of attack and defense. Nature has given to man no other means of sifting the truth, either in religion, law, or politics.

* *

A great deal of indulgence is necessary to strengthen habits of harmony and fraternity.

❧

Let us go on in doing with the pen what in other times was done with the sword, and show that reformation is more practicable by operating on the mind than on the body of man.

❧

It is error alone which needs the support of government. Truth can stand by itself.

❧

Ignorance and bigotry, like other insanities, are incapable of self-government.

❧

Every man's reason is his own rightful umpire. This principle, with that of acquiescence in the will of the majority, will preserve us free and prosperous as long as they are sacredly observed.

❧

I can never fear that things will go wrong where common sense has fair play.

❧

The ground of liberty is to be gained by inches, and we must be contented to secure what we can get from time to time and eternally press forward for what is yet to get. It takes time to persuade men to do even what is for their own good.

Time and truth will at length correct error.

*

Nothing gives one person so much advantage over another as to remain always cool and unruffled under all circumstances.

I have great confidence in the common sense of mankind in general.

Where thought is free in its range, we need never fear to hazard what is good in itself.

*

I was bold in the pursuit of knowledge, never fearing to follow truth and reason to whatever results they led, and bearding every authority which stood in their way.

*

There is not a truth existing which I fear or would wish unknown to the whole world.

*

Opinion, and the just maintenance of it, shall never be a crime in my view: nor bring injury on the individual.

Truth is great and will prevail if left to herself. She is proper and sufficient antagonist to error, and has nothing to fear from the conflict, unless, by human interposition, disarmed of her natural weapons, free argument and debate; errors cease to be dangerous when it is permitted freely to contradict them.

Honesty is the first chapter in the book of wisdom.

The greatest honor of a man is in doing good to his fellow men, not in destroying them.

The care of human life and happiness and not their destruction is the first and only legitimate object of good government.

In every country where man is free to think and to speak, differences of opinion will arise from difference of perception, and the imperfection of reason; but these differences when permitted, as in this happy country, to purify themselves by free discussion, are but as passing clouds overspreading our land transiently and leaving our horizon more bright and serene.

The art of life is the art of avoiding pain; and he is the best pilot, who steers clearest of the rocks and shoals with which it is beset.

All . . . being equally free, no one has a right to say what shall be law for the others. Our way is to put these questions to the vote, and to consider that as law for which the majority votes.

Our saviour . . . has taught us to judge the tree by its fruit, and to leave motives to Him who can alone see into them.

I have ever deemed it more honorable and more profitable, too, to set a good example than to follow a bad one.

We are sensible of the duty and expediency of submitting our opinions to the will of the majority, and can wait with patience till they get right if they happen to be at any time wrong.

He alone who walks strict and upright, and who, in matters of opinion, will be contented that others should be as free as himself and acquiesce when his opinion is freely overruled, will attain his object in the end.

JAMES MADISON

4TH PRESIDENT • 1809–1817

Born: March 16, 1751, in Port Conway, Virginia
Died: June 28, 1836, in Montpelier, Virginia

Wife: Dolley Payne Todd

Religion: Episcopalian

Education: College of New Jersey

Other political offices: Orange County Council of Safety, Virginia
Governor's Council, Member of Continental Congress,
Secretary of State

Known as the father of the Constitution, James Madison served as its leading defender and interpreter for fifty years. He introduced into Congress the Bill of Rights as the Constitution's first ten amendments. As president, Madison went to war with England over British harassment of American ships. Madison lived all his life on a five-thousand-acre tobacco farm in Orange County, Virginia.

I go on the principle that a public dept is a public curse.

*

The Constitution of the United States was created by the people of the United States composing the respective states, who alone had the right.

Knowledge will forever govern ignorance; and a people who mean to be their own governors must arm themselves with the power which knowledge gives.

It is universally admitted that a well-instructed people alone can be permanently a free people.

*

In a free government the security for civil right must be the same as for religious rights. It consists in that one case in the multiplicity of interests, and the other in the multiplicity of sects.

*

Always remember that an armed and trained militia is the firmest bulwark of republics—that without standing armies their liberty can never be in danger, nor with large ones safe.

The war has proved . . . that our free Government, like other free Governments, though slow in its early movements, acquires, in its progress, a force proportioned to its freedom.

❧

What is government itself, but the greatest of all reflections on human nature? If men were angels, no government would be necessary. If angels were to govern men, neither external nor internal controls of government would be necessary.

❧

My life has been so much of a public one, that any review of it must mainly consist of the agency which was my lot in public transactions.

❧

Your remark is very just on the subject of Independence. It was not the offspring of a particular man or particular moment. . . . Our forefathers brought with them the germ of Independence in the principle of self-taxation. Circumstances unfolded and perfected it.

❧

A popular government without popular information, or the means of acquiring it, is but a prologue to a farce or a tragedy; or, perhaps both.

❧

It will be of little avail to the people, that the laws are made by men of their own choice, if the laws be so voluminous that they cannot be read, or so incoherent that they cannot be understood.

Liberty is to faction what air is to fire, an ailment without which it instantly expires. But it could not be less folly to abolish liberty, which is essential to political life, because it nourishes faction, than it would be to wish the annihilation to air, which is essential to animal life, because it imparts to fire its destructive agency.

*

The advice nearest to my heart and deepest in my convictions is that the Union of the States be cherished and perpetuated.

*

The capacity of the female mind for studies of the highest order cannot be doubted, having been sufficiently illustrated by its works of genius, of erudition, and of science.

*

It will be a desirable thing to extinguish from the bosom of every member of the community any apprehensions that there are those among his countrymen who wish to deprive them of the liberty for which they valiantly fought and honorably bled.

*

To the press alone, chequered as it is with abuses, the world is indebted for all the triumphs which have been gained by reason and humanity over error and oppression . . . that to the same beneficent source the United States owe much of the lights which conducted them to the ranks of a free and independent nation, and which have improved their political system into a shape so auspicious to their happiness.

JAMES MONROE

5TH PRESIDENT • 1817–1825
Born: April 28, 1758, in Westmoreland County, Virginia
Died: July 4, 1831, in New York, New York

Wife: Elizabeth Kortright

Religion: Episcopalian

Education: College of William and Mary

Other political offices: Member of Continental Congress, U.S.
Senator, Minister to France, Governor of Virginia, Minister to
England, Secretary of State, Secretary of War

The Monroe Doctrine, warning against European interference in
the affairs of the nations of the Americas, was established in James
Monroe's term of office. So popular that he was not opposed in his
bid for a second term, Monroe was the first president to have been
a U.S. senator. His inauguration in 1817 was the first held outdoors.

The best form of government is that which is most likely to prevent the greatest sum of evil.

✣

Our great resources therefore remain untouched for any purpose which may affect the vital interest of the nation. For all such purposes they are inexhaustible. They are more especially to be found in the virtue, patriotism and intelligence of our fellow-citizens, and in the devotion with which they would yield up by any just measure of taxation all their property in support of the rights and honor of their country.

✣

From a just responsibility I will never shrink, calculating with confidence that in my best efforts to promote the public welfare my motives will always be duly appreciated and my conduct be viewed with that candor and indulgence which I have experienced in other stations.

✣

In this great nation there is but one order, that of the people, whose power, by a peculiarly happy improvement of the representative principle, is transferred from them, without impairing in the slightest degree their sovereignty, in the full extent necessary for the purposes of free, enlightened, and efficient government.

✣

If America wants concessions, she must fight for them. We must purchase our power with our blood.

The American continents . . . by the free and independent condition, which they have assumed and maintain, are henceforth not to be considered as subjects for future colonization by any European Power.

⚜

A complete remedy to a political disease is seldom found until something like a crisis occurs, and this is promoted by the abuse of those who have rendered the most important services, and whose characters will bear the test of inquiry.

⚜

In contemplating what we still have to perform, [the] heart of every citizen must expand with joy when he reflects how near our Government has approached to perfection.

⚜

Preparation for war is constant stimulus to suspicion and ill will.

⚜

The right of self-defense never ceases. It is among the most sacred, and alike necessary to nations and to individuals.

⚜

Such, then, being the highly favored condition of our country, it is in the interest of every citizen to maintain it. What are the dangers which menace us? If any exist, they ought to be ascertained and guarded against.

Had the people of the United States been educated in different principles, had they been less intelligent, less independent, or less virtuous, can it be believed that we should have maintained the same steady and consistent career or been blessed with the same success?

Let us by all wise and constitutional measures promote intelligence among the people as the best means of preserving our liberties.

We must support our rights or lose our character, and with it, perhaps, our liberties. A people who fail to do it can scarcely be said to hold a place among independent nations. National honor is national property of the highest value. The sentiment in the mind of every citizen is national strength. It ought therefore to be cherished.

JB

The earth was given to mankind to support the greatest number of which it is capable, and no tribe or people have a right to withhold from the wants of others more than is necessary for their own support and comfort.

* *

A little flattery will support a man through great fatigue.

✍

Peace and good will have been, and will hereafter be, cultivated with all, and by the most faithful regard to justice. They have been dictated by a love of peace, of economy, and an earnest desire to save the lives of our fellow-citizens from that destruction and our country from that devastation which are inseparable from war when it finds us unprepared for it.

✍

I have never dreaded, nor have I ever shunned, in any situation in which I have been placed, making appeals to the virtue and patriotism of my fellow-citizens, well knowing that they could never be made in vain, especially in times of great emergency or for purposes of high national importance.

✍

The talents and virtues which were displayed in that great struggle were a sure presage of all that has since followed. A people who were able to surmount in their infant state such great perils would be more competent as they rose into manhood to repel any which they might meet in their progress.

JOHN QUINCY ADAMS

6TH PRESIDENT • 1825–1829
Born: July 11, 1767, in Braintree, Massachusetts
Died: February 23, 1848, in Washington, D.C.

Wife: Louisa Catherine Johnson

Religion: Unitarian

Education: Harvard College

Other political offices: Secretary to the U.S. Minister to Russia, Minister to the Netherlands, Minister to Prussia, U.S. Senator, Minister to Russia, Peace Commissioner at Treaty of Ghent, Secretary of State, Member of U. S. House of Representatives

The first son of a president to become president, John Quincy Adams was one of the most successful diplomats of his time. Adams was elected by the House of Representatives after he and his opponent, Andrew Jackson, failed to receive a majority of electoral votes. He was the first president to be photographed and the only president to be elected after his term to the House of Representatives, where he served for seventeen years.

Posterity—you will never know how much it has cost my generation to preserve your freedom. I hope you will make good use of it.

Duty is ours; results are God's.

Always vote for principle, though you may vote alone, and you may cherish the sweetest reflection that your vote is never lost.

Individual liberty is individual power, and as the power of a community is a mass compounded of individual powers, the nation which enjoys the most freedom must necessarily be in proportion to its numbers the most powerful nation.

The only temper that honors a nation is that which rises in proportion to the pressure upon it.

Literature has been the charm of my life, and could I have carved out my own fortunes, to literature would be my whole life have been devoted.

America, with the same voice, which spoke herself into existence as a nation, proclaimed to mankind the inextinguishable rights of human nature, and the only lawful foundation of government.

Independence forever!

ॐ

The dominion of man over physical nature has been extended by the invention of our artists. Liberty and law have marched hand in hand. All the purposes of human association have been accomplished as effectively as under any other government on the globe, and a cost little exceeding in a whole generation the expenditure of nations in a single year.

> # The influence of each human being on others in this life is a kind of immortality.

Internal improvements was at once my conscience and my treasure.

ॐ

Above all, let us never forget, in the most fervent heat of our party conflicts, that there is a cause, embracing and transcending all others . . . the cause of our country.

ॐ

All men profess honesty as long as they can. To believe all men honest would be folly. To believe none so is something worse.

Our Constitution professedly rests upon the good sense and attachment of the people. This basis, weak as it may appear, has not yet been found to fail.

⁂

This prosperity of the country, independent of all agency of the Government, is so great that the people have nothing to disturb them but their own waywardness and corruption.

⁂

Why does it follow that women are fitted for nothing but the cares of domestic life, for bearing children and cooking the food for the family? I say women exhibit the most exalted virtue when they depart from the domestic circle and enter on the concerns of their country, of humanity, and of their God.

⁂

Slavery is the great and foul stain upon the North American Union, and it is contemplation worthy of the most exalted soul whether its total abolition is or is not practicable.

⁂

Courage and perseverance have a magical talisman, before which difficulties disappear and obstacles vanish into air.

⁂

If I cannot hope to give satisfaction to my country, I am at least determined to have the approbation of my own reflections.

ANDREW JACKSON

7TH PRESIDENT • 1829–1837
Born: March 15, 1767, in Waxhaw, South Carolina
Died: June 8, 1845, in Nashville, Tennessee

Wife: Rachel Donelson Robards

Religion: Presbyterian

Education: No formal education

Other political offices: Member of U.S. House of Representatives, U.S. Senator, Tennessee Supreme Court Justice, Governor of the Florida Territory

In the election of 1825, Andrew Jackson won the popular vote and the electoral college vote, but not by a majority; John Quincy Adams was then elected president by the House of Representatives. In 1828 Jackson defeated Adams. The first president born in a log cabin, Jackson was the only president who served in both the Revolutionary War and the War of 1812. Jackson was the first president to ride on a railroad train, and at one point in Jackson's presidency in 1835, the United States was debt-free for the only time in its history.

One man with courage makes a majority.

There are no necessary evils in government. Its evils exist only in its abuses. If it would confine itself to equal protection, and, as Heaven does its rains, shower its favors alike on the high and the low, the rich and the poor, it would be an unqualified blessing.

The right of resisting oppression is a natural right.

If he [the president] speaks to Congress, it must be in the language of the truth.

No one need think that the world can be ruled without blood. The civil sword shall and must be red and bloody.

Take time to deliberate; but when the time for action arrives, stop thinking and go in.

I know what I am fit for. I can command a body of men in a rough way; but I am not fit to be President.

There is no pleasure in having nothing to do; the fun is having lots to do and not doing it.

❦

The wisdom of man never yet contrived a system of taxation that would operate with perfect equality.

❦

To the victors belong the spoils.

❦

It was settled by the Constitution, the laws, and the whole practice of the government that the entire executive power is vested in the President of the United States.

❦

It is to be regretted that the rich and powerful too often bend the acts of government to their own selfish purposes.

❦

The brave man inattentive to his duty, is worth little more to his country than the coward who deserts her in the hour of danger.

❦

It is a damn poor mind that can think of only one way to spell a word.

❦

I hope and trust to meet you in Heaven, both white and black—both white and black.

I cannot be intimidated from doing that which my judgment and conscience tell me is right by any earthly power.

> # Never take counsel of your fears.

Any man worth his salt will stick up for what he believes right, but it takes a slightly better man to acknowledge instantly and without reservation that he is in error.

*

Peace, above all things, is to be desired, but blood must sometimes be spilled to obtain it on equable and lasting terms.

*

You must remember, my fellow citizens, that eternal vigilance by the people is the price of liberty, and that you must pay the price if you wish to secure the blessing.

*

If a national debt is considered a national blessing, then we can get on by borrowing. But as I believe it is a national curse, my vow shall be to pay the national debt.

The individual who refuses to defend his rights when called by his Government, deserves to be a slave, and must be punished as an enemy of his country and friend to her foe.

*

Without union our independence and liberty would never have been achieved; without union they never can be maintained. Divided into twenty-four, or even a smaller number, of separate communities, we shall see our internal trade burdened with numberless restraints and exactions; communications between distant points and sections obstructed or cut off; our sons made soldiers to deluge with blood the fields they now till in peace; the mass of our people borne down and impoverished by taxes to support armies and navies, and military leaders at the head of their victorious legions becoming our lawgivers and judges. The loss of liberty follows dissolution of the Union.

*

You know, I never despair. I have confidence in the virtue and good sense of the people. God is just, and while we act faithfully to the Constitution, he will smile and prosper our exertions.

*

I believe that just laws can make no distinction of privilege between the rich and poor, and that when men of high standing attempt to trample upon the rights of the weak, they are the fittest objects for example and punishment. In general, the great can protect themselves, but the poor and humble require the arm and shield of the law.

MARTIN VAN BUREN

8TH PRESIDENT • 1837–1841
Born: December 5, 1782, in Kinderhook, New York
Died: July 24, 1862, in Kinderhook, New York

Wife: Hannah Hoes

Religion: Dutch Reformed

Education: Kinderhook Academy

Other political offices: New York State Senator, New York Attorney General, U.S. Senator, Governor of New York, Secretary of State, Minister to England, Vice President

Martin Van Buren was the first president born in the United States. Known as the Little Magician because he was a consummate politician, he came to power by assembling the Democratic party, thus helping to lay the groundwork of the American party system. The Amistad incident erupted during his presidency. Van Buren chose to collect his $25,000 annual salary in a lump sum totaling $100,000 at the end of his four-year term. He made three unsuccessful bids for reelection for the presidency.

There is a power in public opinion which will not tolerate an incompetent or unworthy man to hold in his weak or wicked hands the lives and fortunes of his fellow citizens.

No evil can result from [slavery's] inhibition more pernicious than its toleration.

I tread in the footsteps of illustrious men, whose superiors it is our happiness to believe are not found on the executive calendar of any country.

It is easier to do a job right than to explain why you didn't.

The people under our system, like the king in a monarchy, never die.

The capacity of the people for self-government, and their willingness, from a high sense of duty and without those exhibitions of coercive power so generally employed in other countries . . . have also been favorably exemplified in the history of the United States.

Most men are not scolded out of their opinion.

Ignorance and vice breed poverty which was as immutable as the seasons.

All communities are apt to look to government for too much . . . but this ought not to be. The framers of our excellent Constitution and the people who approved it with calm and sagacious deliberation . . . wisely judged that the less government interferes with private pursuits the better for the general prosperity. It is not its legitimate object to make men rich or to repair by direct grants of money or legislation in favor of particular pursuits losses not incurred in the public service. . . . Its real duty . . . is to enact and enforce a system of general laws commensurate with, but not exceeding, the objects of its establishment, and to leave every citizen and every interest to reap under its benign protection the rewards of virtue, industry, and prudence.

WILLIAM HENRY HARRISON

9TH PRESIDENT • MARCH 4, 1841–APRIL 4, 1841
Born: February 9, 1773, in Berkeley, Virginia
Died: April 4, 1841, in Washington, D.C.

Wife: Anna Tuthill Symmes

Religion: Episcopalian

Education: Hampden-Sydney College

Other political offices: Secretary of Northwest Territory, Territorial Governor of Indiana, Member of U.S. House of Representatives, U.S. Senator, Minister to Colombia

After giving the longest inaugural address on record, William Henry Harrison caught cold and died from pneumonia thirty-one days after taking office. He was the only president who studied medicine, although he didn't become a doctor. His campaign slogan "Tippecanoe and Tyler, Too" ranks as one of the most memorable in U.S. history. It refers to the victory of Harrison and the nine hundred men under his command over Tecumseh's Indians at the Battle of Tippecanoe; John Tyler was his running mate.

We admit of no government by divine right. . . . The only legitimate right to govern is an express grant of power from the governed.

ৡ⁀

A decent and manly examination of the acts of government should not only be tolerated, but encouraged.

ৡ⁀

Sir, I wish to understand the true principles of the Government. I wish them carried out. I ask nothing more.

ৡ⁀

The chains of military despotism once fastened upon a nation, ages might pass away before they could be shaken off.

I contend that the strongest of all governments is that which is most free.

The American backwoodsman—clad in his hunting shirt, the product of this domestic industry, and fighting for the country he loves, he is more than a match for the vile but splendid mercenary of a European despot.

The people are the best guardians of their own rights and it is the duty of their executive to abstain from interfering in or thwarting the sacred exercise of the lawmaking functions of their government.

ॐ

There is nothing more corrupting, nothing more destructive of the noblest and finest feelings of our nature, than the exercise of unlimited power.

ॐ

The delicate duty of devising schemes of revenue should be left where the Constitution has placed it— with the immediate representatives of the people.

ॐ

The broad foundation upon which our Constitution rests being the people—a breath of theirs having made, as a breath can unmake, change, or modify it— it can be assigned to none of the great divisions of government but to that of democracy. If such is its theory, those who are called upon to administer it must recognize as its leading principle the duty of shaping their measures as to produce the greatest good to the greatest number.

JOHN TYLER

10TH PRESIDENT • 1841–1845

Born: March 29, 1790, in Greenway, Virginia
Died: January 18, 1862, in Richmond, Virginia

Wives: Letitia Christian; Julia Gardiner

Religion: Episcopalian

Education: College of William and Mary

Other political offices: Member of Virginia House of Delegates, Member of U.S. House of Representatives, Member of Virginia State Legislature, Governor of Virginia, U.S. Senator, Vice President

The first vice president to assume office on the death of the president, John Tyler was also the first president whose wife died while he was in office. The playing of "Hail to the Chief" whenever a president appears at a state function was started by Tyler's second wife. Tyler favored pre-emption, which allowed settlers to obtain government land; rejected a national bank bill; and signed the resolution annexing Texas.

The great primary and controlling interest of the American people is union—union not only in the mere forms of government . . . but union founded in an attachment of . . . individuals for each other.

> Popularity, I have always thought, may aptly be compared to a coquette—the more you woo her, the more apt she is to elude your embrace.

Wealth can only be accumulated by the earnings of industry and the savings of frugality.

The prudent capitalist will never adventure his capital . . . if there exists a state of uncertainty as to whether the government will repeal tomorrow what it has enacted today.

For the first time in our history the person elected to the Vice-Presidency of the United States, by the happening of a contingency provided for in the Constitution, has had devolved upon him the Presidential office.

I can never consent to being dictated to.

⚜

While I shall sedulously cultivate the relations of peace and amity with one and all, it will be my most imperative duty to see that the honor of the country shall sustain no blemish.

⚜

A wise and patriotic consistency will never object to the imposition of necessary burdens for useful ends, and true wisdom dictates the resort to such means in order to supply deficiencies in the revenue, rather than to those doubtful expedients which, ultimating in a public debt, serve to embarrass the resources of the country and to lessen its ability to meet any great emergency which may arise.

⚜

It shall be my first and highest duty to preserve unimpaired the free institutions under which we live and transmit them to those who shall succeed me in their full force and vigor.

⚜

The institutions under which we live, my countrymen, secure each person in the perfect enjoyment of all his rights.

JAMES K. POLK

11TH PRESIDENT • 1845–1849

Born: November 2, 1795, in Mecklenburg County, North Carolina
Died: June 15, 1849, in Nashville, Tennessee

Wife: Sarah Childress

Religion: Presbyterian

Education: University of North Carolina

Other political offices: Member of Tennessee State Legislature, Member of U.S. House of Representatives, Speaker of the House, Governor of Tennessee

James K. Polk and his wife, devout Presbyterians, banned dancing, card playing, and alcoholic beverages while he was in the White House. Polk settled the Oregon boundary dispute and signed the Treaty of 1848 with Mexico, which gave the United States control over California, New Mexico, Arizona, Nevada, Utah, and parts of Colorado and Wyomong. Gold was discovered in California during Polk's presidency. He died three months after leaving office.

Peace, plenty, and contentment reign throughout our borders, and our beloved country presents a sublime moral spectacle to the world.

☙

No president who performs his duties faithfully and conscientiously can have any leisure.

☙

Well may the boldest fear and the wisest tremble when incurring responsibilities on which may depend our country's peace and prosperity, and in some degree the hopes and the happiness of the whole human family.

☙

Although . . . the Chief Magistrate must almost of necessity be chosen by a party and stand pledged to its principles and measures, yet in his official action he should not be the President of a part only, but of the whole people of the United States.

☙

Public opinion: May it always perform one of its appropriate offices, by teaching the public functionaries of the state and of the federal Government, that neither shall assume the exercise of powers entrusted by the Constitution to the other.

☙

The people of the United States have no idea of the extent to which the president's time, which ought to be devoted to more important matters, is occupied by the voracious and often unprincipled persons who seek office.

I cannot, whilst president of the United States, descend to enter into a newspaper controversy.

*

In truth, though I occupy a very high position, I am the hardest working man in this country.

We must ever mandate the principle that the people of this continent alone have the right to decide their own destiny.

The Constitution itself, plainly written as it is, the safeguard of our federative compact, the offspring of concession and compromise, binding together in the bonds of peace and union this great and increasing family of free and independent States, will be the chart by which I shall be directed.

*

I am heartily rejoiced that my term is so near its close. I will soon cease to be a servant and will become a sovereign.

I prefer to supervise the whole operations of the Government myself rather than entrust the public business to subordinates and this makes my duties great.

Genius is free to announce its inventions and discoveries, and the hand is free to accomplish whatever the head conceives not incompatible with the rights of a fellow being. All distinctions of birth or of rank have been abolished. All citizens, whether native or adopted, are placed upon terms of precise equality. All are entitled to equal rights and equal protection. No union exists between church and state, and perfect freedom of opinion is guaranteed to all sects and creeds.

ZACHARY TAYLOR

12TH PRESIDENT • 1849–1850
Born: November 24, 1784, in Barboursville, Virginia
Died: July 9, 1850, in Washington, D.C.

Wife: Margaret Mackall Smith

Religion: Episcopalian

Education: No formal education

Other political offices: None

The second president to die in office, Zachary Taylor was elected in the first presidential election in which each state election was held on the same day. A hero in the Mexican War, Old Rough and Ready was a career soldier. He worked to have California admitted to the union as a free state, even though he had once been a slaveholder. Taylor died five days after taking part in a ceremony at the Washington Monument on a hot Fourth of July.

It would be judicious to act with magnanimity towards a prostrate foe.

> The axe, pick, saw, and trowel, has become more the implement of the American soldier than the cannon, musket or sword.

As American freemen we cannot but sympathize in all efforts to extend the blessings of civil and political liberty, but at the same time we are warned by the admonitions of history and the voice of our beloved Washington to abstain from entangling alliances with foreign nations.

For more than half a century, during which kingdoms and empires have fallen, this Union has stood unshaken. The patriots who formed it have long since descended to the grave; yet still it remains, the proudest monument to their memory.... In my judgment, its dissolution would be the greatest of calamities.... Upon its preservation must depend our own happiness and that of countless generations to come. Whatever dangers may threaten it, I shall stand by it and maintain it in its integrity to the full extent of the obligations imposed and the power conferred upon me by the Constitution.

Chosen by the body of the people under the assurance that my Administration would be devoted to the welfare of the whole country, and not to the support of any particular section or merely local interest, I this day renew the declarations I have heretofore made and proclaim my fixed determination to maintain to the extent of my ability the Government in its original purity and to adopt as the basis of my public policy those great republican doctrines which constitute the strength of our national existence.

In conclusion I congratulate you, my fellow citizens, upon the high state of prosperity to which the goodness of Divine Providence has conducted our common country. Let us invoke a continuance of the same protecting care which has led us from small beginnings to the eminence we this day occupy, and let us seek to deserve that continuance by prudence and moderation in our councils, by well-directed attempts to assuage the bitterness which too often marks unavoidable differences of opinion, by the promulgation and practice of just and liberal principles, and by an enlarged patriotism, which shall acknowledge no limits but those of our own widespread Republic.

I have always done my duty. I am ready to die. My only regret is for the friends I leave behind.

MILLARD FILLMORE

13TH PRESIDENT • 1850–1853
Born: Jan. 7, 1800, in Locke Township, New York
Died: March 8, 1874, in Buffalo, New York

Wife: Abigail Powers

Religion: Unitarian

Education: No formal education

Other political offices: Member of New York State Assembly,
Member of U.S. House of Representatives, Comptroller of New
York, Vice President

The son of poor farmers, Millard Fillmore took office after the death
of Zachary Taylor. Fillmore was largely self-taught, first becoming a
lawyer and then a politician. Fillmore dispatched Commodore Perry
to open Japan to Western trade. The White House's first library, bath-
tub, and kitchen stove were installed while Fillmore was in office.
After his term, he became chancellor of the University of Buffalo.

An honorable defeat is better than a dishonorable victory.

❧

God knows I detest slavery.

❧

I would submit that the best way to avoid a war with Great Britain is to show her that we are prepared to meet her.

The man who can look upon a crisis without being willing to offer himself upon the altar of his country is not fit for public trust.

The majority possesses all the power, the minority have nothing to protect them but the Constitution and the Rules of the House.

❧

We should act to other countries as we wish them to act towards us.

❧

The law is the only sure protection of the weak and the only efficient restraint upon the strong.

* *

It is not strange . . . to mistake change for progress.

❧

I have no hostility to foreigners. . . . Having witnessed their deplorable condition in the old country, God forbid I should add to their sufferings by refusing them an asylum in this.

❧

The government of the United States is a limited government. It is confined to the exercise of powers expressly granted, and such others as may be necessary for carrying those powers into effect; and it is at all times an especial duty to guard against any infringement on the just rights of the states.

❧

It is a national disgrace that our presidents . . . should be cast adrift, and perhaps be compelled to keep a corner grocery for subsistence. . . . We elect a man to the presidency, expect him to be honest, to give up a lucrative profession, perhaps, and after we have done with him we let him go into seclusion and perhaps poverty.

❧

I had not the advantage of a classical education, and no man should, in my judgment, accept a degree he cannot read.

❧

Let us remember that revolutions do not always establish freedom. Our own free institutions were not the offspring of our Revolution.

FRANKLIN PIERCE

14TH PRESIDENT • 1853–1857

Born: November 23, 1804, in Hillsborough, New Hampshire
Died: October 8, 1869, in Concord, New Hampshire

Wife: Jane Means Appleton

Religion: Episcopalian

Education: Bowdoin College

Other political offices: Member of New Hampshire State Legislature, Member of U.S. House of Representatives, U.S. Senator

As president, Franklin Pierce approved the Kansas-Nebraska Act, which permitted territories to decide whether to allow slavery. This led to bloody fighting and eventually the Civil War. Pierce was the first elected president not renominated by his own party for reelection.

We have nothing in our history or position to invite aggression; we have everything to beckon us to the cultivation of relations of peace and amity with all nations.

☙

The maintenance of large standing armies in our country would be not only dangerous, but unnecessary.

☙

The stars upon your banner have become nearly threefold their original number; your densely populated possessions skirt the shores of the two great oceans.

☙

So long as [the American citizen] can discern every star in its place upon that ensign, without wealth to purchase for him preferment or title to purchase for him place, it will be his privilege, and must be his acknowledged right, to stand unabashed even in the presence of princes, with a proud consciousness that he is himself one of a nation of sovereigns.

☙

It is a relief to feel that no heart but my own can know the personal regret and bitter sorrow over which I have been borne to a position so suitable for others rather than desirable for myself.

☙

A Republic without parties is a complete anomaly. The history of all popular governments shows how absurd is the idea of their attempting to exist without parties.

We have to maintain inviolate the great doctrine of
the inherent right of popular self-government, to
render cheerful obedience to the laws of the land, to
unite in enforcing their execution, and to frown
indignantly on all combinations to resist them; to
preserve sacred from all touch of usurpation, as the
very palladium of our political salvation, the reserved
rights and powers of the several States and the people.

The storm of frenzy and faction
must inevitably dash itself in
vain against the unshaken rock
of the Constitution.

The circumstances under which I have been called for
a limited period to preside over the destinies of the
Republic fill me with a profound sense of
responsibility, but with nothing like shrinking
apprehension. I repair to the post assigned me not as
to one sought, but in obedience to the unsolicited
expression of your will, answerable only for a fearless,
faithful, and diligent exercise of my best powers. I
ought to be, and am, truly grateful for the rare
manifestation of the nation's confidence; but this, so
far from lightening my obligations, only adds to their
weight. You have summoned me in my weakness; you
must sustain me by your strength.

But let not the foundation of our hope rest upon man's wisdom. It will not be sufficient that sectional prejudices find no place in the public deliberations. It will not be sufficient that the rash counsels of human passion are rejected. It must be felt that there is no national security but in the nation's humble, acknowledged dependence upon God and His overruling providence.

We have been carried in safety through a perilous crisis. Wise counsels, like those which gave us the Constitution, prevailed to uphold it. Let the period be remembered as an admonition, and not as an encouragement, in any section of the Union, to make experiments where experiments are fraught with such fearful hazard. Let it be impressed upon all hearts that, beautiful as our fabric is, no earthly power or wisdom could ever reunite its broken fragments. Standing as I do, almost within view of the green slopes of Monticello, and, as it were, within reach of the tomb of Washington, with all the cherished memories of the past gathering around me like so many eloquent voices of exhortation from heaven, I can express no better hope for my country than that the kind Providence which smiled upon our fathers may enable their children to preserve the blessings they have inherited.

JAMES BUCHANAN

15TH PRESIDENT • 1857–1861

Born: April 23, 1791, in Cove Gap, Pennsylvania
Died: June 1, 1868, in Wheatland, Pennsylvania

Wife: Not married

Religion: Presbyterian

Education: Dickinson College

Other political offices: Member of Pennsylvania House of
Representatives, Member of U. S. House of Representatives,
Minister to Russia, U.S. Senator, Secretary of State, Minister to
England

James Buchanan's term as president was overshadowed by the
national debate over slavery. Great hopes that Buchanan would be
able to unite the nation were dashed by his passivity, which led to
Lincoln's election and the secession of seven states in the Lower
South. Buchanan was the only president to never marry, and his
niece Harriet Lane served as White House hostess during his term.

Our union rests upon public opinion, and can never be cemented by the blood of its citizens shed in civil war.

The distribution of patronage of the Government is by far the most disagreeable duty of the President. Applicants are so numerous, and their applications are pressed with such eagerness by their friends both in and out of Congress, that the selection of one for any desirable office gives offense to many.

Constitutions are restraints imposed, not by arbitrary authority, but by people upon themselves and their own representatives.

From Caesar to Cromwell, and from Cromwell to Napoleon . . . history presents the same solemn warning—beware of elevating to the highest civil trust the commander of our victorious armies.

Whatever the result may be, I shall carry to my grave the consciousness that I at least meant well for my country.

It is our glory that whilst other nations have extended their dominion by the sword we have never acquired any territory except by fair purchase or, as in the case of Texas, by the voluntary determination of a brave, kindred, and independent people to blend their destinies with our own.

Capital and capitalists . . . are proverbially timid.

Liberty must be allowed to work out its natural results; and these will, ere long, astonish the world.

What is right and what is practicable are two different things.

❧

What sir, prevent the American people from crossing the Rocky Mountains? You might as well command Niagara not to flow. We must fulfill our destiny.

❧

Public virtue is the vital spirit of republics, and history proves that when this has decayed and the love of money has usurped its place, although the forms of free government may remain for a season, the substance has departed forever.

❧

The voice of the majority, speaking in the manner prescribed by the Constitution, was heard, and instant submission followed. Our own country could alone have exhibited so grand and striking a spectacle of the capacity of man for self-government.

There is nothing stable but Heaven and the Constitution.

இ

To avoid entangling alliances has been a maxim of our policy ever since the days of Washington, and its wisdom no one will attempt to dispute.

இ

No nation in the tide of time has ever been blessed with so rich and noble an inheritance as we enjoy in the public lands. In administering this important trust, whilst it may be wise to grant portions of them for the improvement of the remainder, yet we should never forget that it is our cardinal policy to reserve these lands, as much as may be, for actual settlers, and this at moderate prices. We shall thus not only best promote the prosperity of the new States and Territories, by furnishing them a hardy and independent race of honest and industrious citizens, but shall secure homes for our children and our children's children, as well as those exiles from foreign shores who may seek in this country to improve their condition and to enjoy the blessings of civil and religious liberty. Such emigrants have done much to promote the growth and prosperity of the country. They have proved faithful both in peace and in war. After becoming citizens they are entitled, under the constitution and laws, to be placed on a perfect equality with native-born citizens, and in their character they should ever be kindly recognized.

ABRAHAM LINCOLN

16TH PRESIDENT • 1861–1865

Born: February 12, 1809, in Hardin County, Kentucky
Died: April 15, 1865, in Washington, D.C.

Wife: Mary Todd Lincoln

Religion: No formal affiliation

Education: No formal education

Other political offices: Member of Illinois State Legislature, Member of U.S. House of Representatives

Born dirt-poor in a log cabin in Kentucky, Abraham Lincoln was largely self-educated. In his campaign, he firmly expressed his opposition to slavery, and upon his election, seven slave-holding states left the Union to form the Confederate States of America. Midway through the Civil War, Lincoln issued the Emancipation Proclamation, which freed all slaves in the Confederacy. Lincoln was the first president to die by assassination.

★ ★

There is something back of these, entwining itself more closely about the human heart. That something is the principle of "Liberty to all"—the principle that clears the path for all, gives hope to all, and, by consequence, enterprise and industry to all.

Stand with anybody that stands right. Stand with him while he is right, and part with him when he goes wrong.

Allow me to say that you, as a portion of the great American people, need only to maintain your composure, stand up to your sober convictions of right, to your obligations of right, to your obligations to the Constitution, and act in accordance with those sober convictions, and the clouds now on the horizon will be dispelled, and we shall have a bright and glorious future.

Work, work, work, is the main thing.

It is decreed that I should go down because of this speech, then let me go down linked to the truth—let me die in the advocacy of what is just and right.

I do not state a thing and say I know it when I do not . . . I mean to put a case no stronger than the truth will allow.

At every step we must be true to the main purpose.

ॐ

Half-finished work generally proves to be labor lost.

ॐ

Although volume upon volume is written to prove slavery a good thing, we never hear of the man who wishes to take the good of it, by being a slave himself.

ॐ

Let every American, every lover of liberty, every well-wisher to his posterity, swear by the blood of the Revolution never to violate in the least particular the laws of the country, and never to tolerate their violation by others.

ॐ

I am a slow walker, but I never walk back.

My great concern is not whether you have failed, but whether you are content with your failure.

I believe the declaration that "all men are created equal" is the great fundamental principle upon which our free institutions rest.

★ ★

I do not consider that I have ever accomplished anything without God; and if it is His will that I must die by the hand of an assassin, I must be resigned. I must do my duty as I see it, and leave the rest with God.

❧

Important principles may and must be inflexible.

❧

No men living are more worthy to be trusted that those who toil up from poverty—none less inclined to take, or touch, aught which they have not honestly earned.

❧

He has a right to criticize, who has a heart to help.

❧

It was the oath I took that I would, to the best of my ability, preserve, protect, and defend the Constitution of the United States. I could not take the office without taking the oath.

❧

Nor was it my view that I might take an oath to get power, and break the oath in using the power.

❧

Let us have faith that right makes might.

❧

I have an irrepressible desire to live till I can be assured that the world is a little better for my having lived in it.

I don't know but that God has created some one man great enough to comprehend the whole of this stupendous crisis and transaction from beginning to end, and endowed him with sufficient wisdom to manage and direct it. I confess I do not fully understand, and foresee it all. But I am placed here where I am obliged to the best of my poor ability to deal with it.

❧

Nearly all men can stand adversity, but if you want to test a man's character, give him power.

❧

I am decided; my course is fixed; my path is blazed. The Union and the Constitution shall be preserved and the laws enforced at every and at all hazards. I expect the people to sustain me. They have never yet forsaken any true man.

❧

Tact is the ability to describe others as they see themselves.

❧

What is it that we hold most dear amongst us? Our own liberty and prosperity. What has ever threatened our liberty and prosperity, save and except this institution of slavery?

❧

I made a point of honor and conscience in all things to stick to my word, especially if others had been induced to act on it.

Towering genius disdains a beaten path.

The world has never had a good definition of the word liberty, and the American people, just now, are much in want of one. We all declare for liberty; but in using the same word we do not all mean the same thing. With some the word liberty may mean for each man to do as he pleases with himself, and the product of his labor; while with others the same word may mean for some men to do as they please with other men, and the product of other men's labor. Here are two, not only different, but incompatible things, called by the same name, liberty.

A man's character is like a tree and his reputation like its shadow; the shadow is what we think of it; the tree is the real thing.

My friends, I have detained you about as long as I desired to do, and I have only to say, let us discard all this quibbling about this man and the other man—this race and that race being inferior, and therefore they must be placed in an inferior position. Let us discard all these things, and unite as one people throughout this land, until we shall once more stand up declaring that all men are created equal.

I want every man to have a chance, and I believe a black man is entitled to it—in which he can better his condition.

I am a living witness that any one of your children may look to come here [the White House] as my father's child has.

❦

Our government rests in public opinion. Whoever can change public opinion can change the government.

❦

I have never had a feeling, politically, that did not spring from the sentiments embodied in the Declaration of Independence.

❦

Most government has been based, practically, on the denial of the equal rights of men . . . ours began by affirming those rights.

❦

I am exceedingly anxious that this Union, the Constitution, and the liberties of the people shall be perpetuated in accordance with the original idea for which that struggle was made, and I shall be most happy indeed if I shall be an humble instrument in the hands of the Almighty, and of this, His almost chosen people, for perpetuating the object of that great struggle.

❦

I am very little inclined on any occasion to say anything unless I hope to produce some good by it.

The ballot is stronger than the bullet.

A house divided against itself cannot stand. I believe this government cannot endure permanently half slave and half free.

You can fool all of the people some of the time, and some of the people all of the time, but you cannot fool all of the people all of the time.

On the whole, my impression is that mercy bears richer fruits than any other attribute.

Fellow citizens, we cannot escape history.

Our reliance is the love of liberty which God has planted in our bosoms. Our defense is in the preservation of the spirit which prized liberty as the heritage of all men, in all lands, everywhere. Destroy this spirit and you have planted the seeds of despotism around your own doors. Familiarize yourselves with the chains of bondage, and you are preparing your own limbs to wear them.

The fiery trial through which we pass will light us
down in honor or dishonor to the last generation. We
say we are for the Union. The world will not forget that
we say this. We know how to save it. We, even we here,
hold the power and bear the responsibility. In giving
freedom to the slave, we assure freedom to the free—
honorable alike is what we give and what we preserve.
We shall nobly save or meanly lose the last, best hope
of Earth. Other means may succeed; this could not fail.
The way is plain, peaceful, generous, just a way which if
followed the world will forever applaud and God must
forever bless.

꧁

Common-looking people are the best in the world:
that is the reason the Lord makes so many of them.

꧁

I wish some of you would tell me the brand of whiskey
that Grant drinks. I would like to send a barrel of it to
my other generals.

꧁

Truth is generally the best vindication against slander.

꧁

With malice toward none, charity for all, with
firmness in the right as God gives us to see the right,
let us strive on to finish the work we are in, to bind up
the nation's wounds, to care for him who shall have
borne the battle and for his widow and his orphan, to
do all which may achieve and cherish a just and lasting
peace among ourselves and with all nations.

★ ★

It is best not to swap horses while crossing the river.

❧

I am always for the man who wishes to work.

❧

Fourscore and seven years ago our fathers brought forth on this continent a new nation, conceived in liberty, and dedicated to the proposition that all men are created equal. Now we are engaged in a great civil war, testing whether that nation or any nation so conceived and so dedicated can long endure. We are met on a great battlefield of that war. We have come to dedicate a portion of that field as a final resting place for those who here gave their lives that that nation might live. It is altogether fitting and proper that we should do this. But in a larger sense, we cannot dedicate—we cannot consecrate—we cannot hallow—this ground. The brave men, living and dead, who struggled here, have consecrated it far above our poor power to add or detract. The world will little note nor long remember what we say here, but it can never forget what they did here. It is for us, the living, rather to be dedicated here to the unfinished work which they who fought here have thus far so nobly advanced. It is rather for us to be here dedicated to the great task remaining before us—that from these honored dead we take increased devotion to that cause for which they gave the last full measure of devotion; that we here highly resolve that these dead shall not have died in vain; that this nation, under God, shall have a new birth of freedom; and that government of the people, by the people, for the people, shall not perish from the earth.

★ ★

I don't know who my grandfather was; I am much more concerned to know what his grandson will be.

Always bear in mind that your own resolution to succeed is more important than any other one thing.

I now leave, not knowing whether ever I may return, with a task before me greater than that which rested upon Washington. Without the assistance of that Divine Being who attended him, I cannot succeed. With that assistance, I cannot fail.

The union must be preserved, and hence, all indispensable means must be employed.

I think of the whole people of this nation; they will ever do well if well done by.

If you make a bad bargain, hug it all the tighter.

Persuade your neighbor to compromise whenever you can.

If you would win a man to your cause, first convince
him that you are his sincere friend. Therein is a drop
of honey that catches his heart, which . . . when gained,
you will find but little trouble in convincing his
judgment of the justice of your cause.

❧

Bad promises are better broken than kept.

❧

It is true . . . that very great responsibility rests upon
me in the position to which the votes of the American
people have called me. I am deeply sensible of the
weighty responsibility . . . I turn, then, and look to the
American people, and to that God who has never
forsaken them.

❧

If the people remain right, your public men can never
betray you. Cultivate and protect that sentiment [that
the principles of liberty are eternal] and your
ambitious leaders will be reduced to the position of
servants instead of masters.

❧

It was a common notion that those who laughed heartily
and often never amounted to much—never made great
men. If this be the case, farewell to all my glory.

❧

The probability that we may fall in the struggle ought
not to deter us from the support of a cause we believe
to be just.

The way for a young man to rise, is to improve himself every way he can, never suspecting that anybody wishes to hinder him. Allow me to assure you, that suspicion and jealousy never did help any man in any situation. There may sometimes be ungenerous attempts to keep a young man down; and they will succeed, too, if he allows his whole mind to be diverted from its true channel to brood over the attempted injury.

No matter how much cats fight, there always seems to be plenty of kittens.

We are indeed going through a trial—a fiery trial. In the very responsible position in which I happen to be placed, being a humble instrument in the hands of our Heavenly Father, as I am and as we all are, to work out His great purposes, I have desired that all my works and acts may be according to His will, and that it might be so, I have sought His aid—but if after endeavoring to do my best in the light which He affords me, I find my efforts fail, I must believe that for some purpose unknown to me, He wills it otherwise.

Better to remain silent and to be thought a fool than to speak out and remove all doubt.

While the people retain their virtue and vigilance, no administration by any extreme of wickedness or folly can very seriously injure the government in the short space of four years.

By general law, life and limb must be protected, yet often a limb must be amputated to have a life; but a life is never wisely given to save a limb. I felt that measures otherwise unconstitutional might become lawful by becoming indispensable to the preservation of the Constitution through the preservation of the nation. Right or wrong, I assumed this ground and now avow it.

I have never tried to conceal my opinions, nor tried to deceive anyone in reference to them.

Universal idleness would speedily result in universal ruin.

Determine that the thing can and shall be done, and then we shall find the way.

Adhere to your purpose and you will soon feel as well as you ever did. On the contrary, if you falter, and give up, you will lose the power to keep any resolution, and will regret it all your life. Take the advice of a friend . . . and stick to your purpose.

I am a firm believer in the people. If given the truth, they can be depended upon to meet any national crisis. The great point is to bring them the real facts.

I claim not to have controlled events, but confess plainly that events have controlled me.

M·

Most folks are about as happy as they make up their minds to be.

M·

It is, fellow-citizens, for the whole American people, and not for one single man alone, to advance the great cause of the Union and the Constitution. And in a country like this, where every man bears on his face the marks of intelligence, where every man's clothing, if I may so speak, shows signs of comfort, and every dwelling signs of happiness and contentment, where schools and churches abound on every side, the Union can never be in danger.

M·

The fight must go on. The cause of civil liberty must not be surrendered at the end of one or even one hundred defeats.

M·

I have often inquired of myself, what great principle or idea it was that kept this confederacy so long together. It was not the mere matter of the separation of the colonies from the motherland; but something in that Declaration giving liberty, not alone to the people of this country, but hope to the world for all future time. It was that which gave promise that in due time the weights should be lifted from the shoulders of all men, and that all should have an equal chance.

If the politicians and leaders of parties were as true as the people, there would be little fear that the peace of the country would be disturbed. I have been selected to fill an important office for a brief period, and am now, in your eyes, invested with an influence which will soon pass away; but should my administration prove to be a very wicked one, or what is more probably, a very foolish one, if you, the people, are but true to yourselves and to the Constitution, there is but little harm I can do, thank God.

જી

Laughter is the joyous, beautiful, universal evergreen of life.

જી

Let us readopt the Declaration of Independence, and with it the practices and policy which harmonize with it. Let North and South—let all Americans—let all lovers of liberty everywhere join in the great and good work. If we do this, we shall not only have saved the Union, but we shall have so saved it as to make and to keep it forever worthy of the saving. We shall have so saved it that the succeeding millions of free happy people, the world over, shall rise up and call us blessed to the latest generations.

જી

Human nature will not change. In any future great national trial, compared with the men of this, we shall have as weak and as strong, as silly and as wise, as bad and as good. Let us therefore study the incidents of this, as philosophy to learn wisdom from, and none of them as wrongs to be revenged.

We proposed to give all a chance; and we expect the weak to grow stronger, the ignorant, wiser, and all better, and happier together.

It is not the qualified voters, but the qualified voters who choose to vote, that constitute the political power of the State.

*

It is difficult to make a man miserable when he feels worthy of himself and claims kindred to the great God who made him.

*

The loss of enemies does not compensate for the loss of friends.

*

But this government must be preserved in spite of the acts of any man or set of men. It is worthy of your every effort. Nowhere in the world is presented a government of so much liberty and equality. To the humblest and poorest amongst us are held out the highest privileges and positions. The present moment finds me at the White House, yet there is as good a chance for your children as there was for my father's.

The integrity of our country and the stability of our government mainly depend . . . on the loyalty, virtue, patriotism, and intelligence of the American people.

Let us be quite sober. Let us diligently apply the means, never doubting that a just God, in his own good time, will give us the rightful result.

We thereby restore the national faith, the national confidence, the national feeling of brotherhood. We thereby reinstate the spirit of concession and compromise—that spirit which has never failed us in past perils, and which may be safely trusted for all the future.

The struggle of today is not altogether for today—it is for a vast future also.

The power of hope upon the human exertion and happiness is wonderful.

Quarrel not at all. No man resolved to make the most of himself can spare time for personal contention. Still less can he afford to take all the consequences, including the vitiating of his temper and the loss of self-control. Yield larger things to which you can show no more than equal right; and yield lesser ones, though clearly your own. Better give your path to a dog than be bitten by him in contesting for the right. Even killing the dog would not cure the bite.

Let every man remember that to violate the law is to trample on the blood of his father, and to tear the charter of his own and his children's liberty.

The better part of one's life consists of his friendships.

❧

I intend no modification of my oft-expressed personal wish that all men everywhere could be free.

❧

In all our rejoicings, let us neither express nor cherish any hard feelings toward any citizen who, by his vote, has differed with us. Let us at all times remember that all American citizens are brothers of common country, and should do well together in the bonds of fraternal feeling.

❧

Always bear in mind that your own resolution to succeed is more important than any other one thing.

❧

By all means, don't say "if I can": say "I will."

❧

If you intend to go to work, there is no better place than right where you are.

Those who deny freedom deserve it not for
themselves; and under a just God, cannot long retain it.

Upon the subject of education, not presuming to
dictate any plan or system respecting it, I can only say
that I view it as the most important subject which we as
a people can be engaged in.

I am glad of all the support I can get anywhere, if I can
get it without practicing any deception to obtain it.

Men are not flattered by being shown that there has
been a difference of purpose between the Almighty
and them.

As I would not be a slave, so I would not be a master.
This expresses my idea of democracy. Whatever differs
from this, to the extent of the difference, is no
democracy.

I go for all sharing the privileges of the government
who assist in bearing its burdens, by no means
excluding women.

The world shall know that I will keep my faith to
friends and enemies, come what will.

ANDREW JOHNSON

17TH PRESIDENT • 1865–1869

Born: December 29, 1808, in Raleigh, North Carolina
Died: July 31, 1875, in Carter's Station, Tennessee

Wife: Eliza McCardle

Religion: No formal affiliation

Education: No formal education

Other political offices: Alderman of Greenville, Tennessee; Mayor of Greenville, Tennessee; Member of Tennessee State Legislature; Member of U.S. House of Representatives; Governor of Tennessee; U.S. Senator; Vice President

Born to an extremely poor family in Raleigh, Andrew Johnson never attended school, but was a trained tailor. He became president when Lincoln was shot. Johnson battled with Congress over the reconstruction of the South after the Civil War and was impeached by the House in 1868 for illegally firing his war secretary. The Senate later acquitted him.

Honest conviction is my courage; the Constitution is my guide.

❧

The goal is to strive for a poor government but a rich people.

❧

I hold it the duty of the executive to insist upon frugality in the expenditure, and a sparing economy is itself a great national source.

❧

There are some who lack confidence in the integrity and capacity of the people to govern themselves. To all who entertain such fears I will most respectfully say that I entertain none . . . if man is not capable, and is not to be trusted with the government of himself, is he to be trusted with the government of others . . . who, then, will govern? The answer must be, Man—for we have no angels in the shape of men, as yet, who are willing to take charge of our political affairs.

❧

I know that sincere philanthropy is earnest for the immediate realization of its remotest aims; but time is always an element in reform. It is one of the greatest acts on record to have brought 4,000,000 people into freedom. The career of free industry must be fairly opened to them, and then their future prosperity and condition must, after all, rest mainly on themselves. If they fail, and so perish away, let us be careful that the failure shall not be attributable to any denial of justice.

Legislation can neither be wise nor just which seeks the welfare of a single interest at the expense and to the injury of many and varied interests.

⁊

It is plain that an indefinite or permanent exclusion of any part of the country from representation must be attended by a spirit of disquiet and complaint. It is unwise and dangerous to pursue a course of measures which will unite a very large section of the country against another section of the country, however much the latter may preponderate.

If I am shot at, I want no man to be in the way of the bullet.

I have performed my duty to God, my country, and my family. I have nothing to fear in approaching death. To me it is the mere shadow of God's protecting wing. . . . Here I will rest in quiet and peace beyond the reach of calumny's poisoned shaft, the influence of envy and jealous enemies, where treason and traitors or State backsliders and hypocrites in church can have no peace.

⁊

It is our sacred duty to transmit unimpaired to our posterity the blessings of liberty which were bequeathed to us by the founders of the Republic.

The Union of the United States of America was intended by its authors to last as long as the States themselves shall last.

❧

Our Government springs from and was made for the people—not the people for the Government. To them it owes allegiance; from them it must derive its courage, strength, and wisdom.

❧

To express gratitude to God in the name of the people for the preservation of the United States is my first duty in addressing you. Our thoughts next revert to the death of the late President by an act of parricidal treason. The grief of the nation is still fresh. It finds some solace in the consideration that he lived to enjoy the highest proof of confidence by entering on the renewed term of the Chief Magistracy to which he had been elected; that he brought the civil war substantially to a close; that his loss was deplored in all parts of the Union; and that foreign nations have rendered justice to his memory. His removal cast upon me a heavier weight of cares than ever devolved upon any one of his predecessors. To fulfill my trust I need the support and confidence of all who are associated with me in the various departments of Government and the support and confidence of the people. There is but one way in which I can hope to gain their necessary aid. It is to state with frankness the principles which guide my conduct, and their application to the present state of affairs, well aware that the efficiency of my labors will in a great measure depend on your and their undivided approbation.

ULYSSES S. GRANT

18TH PRESIDENT • 1869–1877

Born: April 27, 1822, in Point Pleasant, Ohio
Died: July 23, 1885, in Mount McGregor, New York

Wife: Julia Boggs Dent

Religion: Methodist

Education: West Point

Other political offices: None

As the commander of the Union armies during the Civil War, Ulysses S. Grant became a national hero. During his terms, Grant supported the amendment that gave blacks the right to vote and continued federal occupation of the South. His administration was plagued with a series of bribery scandals.

The friend in my adversity I shall always cherish most. I can better trust those who helped to relieve the gloom of my dark hours than those who are so ready to enjoy with me the sunshine of my prosperity.

One of my superstitions had always been when I started to go anywhere, or to do anything, not to turn back, or stop until the thing intended was accomplished.

God gave us Lincoln and liberty. Let's fight for both.

No terms except unconditional and immediate surrender can be accepted.

I know no method to secure the repeal of bad or obnoxious laws so effective as their stringent execution.

Keep the church and State forever separate.

The country having just emerged from a great rebellion, many questions will come before it for settlement in the next four years which preceding Administrations have never had to deal with. In meeting these it is desirable that they should be approached calmly, without prejudice, hate, or sectional pride, remembering that the greatest good to the greatest number is the object to be attained.

★ ★

To maintain peace in the future it is necessary to be prepared for war.

*

I shall on all subjects have a policy to recommend, but none to enforce against the will of the people.

*

There never was a time when, in my opinion, some way could not be found to prevent the drawing of the sword.

*

I have acted in every instance from a conscientious desire to do what was right. . . . Failures have been errors of judgment, not of intent.

*

The right of revolution is an inherent one. When people are oppressed by their government, it is a natural right they enjoy to relieve themselves of oppression, if they are strong enough, whether by withdrawal from it, or by overthrowing it and substituting a government more acceptable.

*

It was my fortune, or misfortune, to be called to the office of Chief Executive without any previous political training.

*

I never advocated war except as a means of peace.

*

Labor disgraces no man, but occasionally men disgrace labor.

The fact is I think I am a verb instead of a personal pronoun. A verb is anything that signifies to be; to do; or to suffer. I signify all three.

I know only two tunes: one of them is "Yankee Doodle" and the other one isn't.

The war is over—the rebels are our countrymen again.

I never learned to swear . . . I could never see the use of swearing . . . I have always noticed . . . that swearing helps rouse a man's anger.

The responsibilities of the position I feel, but accept them without fear.

The young men of the country—those who from their age must be its rulers twenty-five years hence—have a peculiar interest in maintaining the national honor. A moment's reflection as to what will be our commanding influence among the nations of the earth in their day, if they are only true to themselves, should inspire them with national pride. All divisions—geographical, political, and religious—can join in this common sentiment.

Let no guilty man escape, if it can be avoided. No personal considerations should stand in the way of performing a duty.

*

The theory of government changes with general progress. Now that the telegraph is made available for communicating thought, together with rapid transit by steam, all parts of a continent are made contiguous for all purposes of government, and communication between the extreme limits of the country made easier than it was throughout the old thirteen States at the beginning of our national existence.

*

Social equality is not a subject to be legislated upon.

*

The art of war is simple enough. Find our where your enemy is. Get at him as soon as you can. Strike at him as hard as you can, and keep moving on.

*

It is probably well that we had the war when we did. We are better off now than we would have been without it, and have made more rapid progress than we otherwise should have made.

*

It is not probable that public affairs will ever again receive attention from me further than as a citizen of the Republic, always taking a deep interest in the honor, integrity, and prosperity of the whole land.

RUTHERFORD B. HAYES

19TH PRESIDENT • 1877–1881
Born: October 4, 1822, in Delaware, Ohio
Died: January 17, 1893, in Fremont, Ohio

Wife: Lucy Ware Webb

Religion: No formal affiliation

Education: Kenyon College, Harvard Law School

Other political offices: Member of U.S. House of Representatives, Governor of Ohio

Rutherford B. Hayes was the only president to have been wounded while serving in the Civil War. Although he won neither the popular nor electoral vote, he was awarded disputed electoral votes by an electoral commission and became president. He was the first president to have graduated from law school and the first to visit the West Coast while in office. During Hayes's term, federal troops were withdrawn from the South, ending Reconstruction.

It is now true that this is God's Country, if equal rights—a fair start and an equal chance in the race of life are everywhere secured to all.

※

Nobody ever left the presidency with less regret, less disappointment, fewer heart burnings, or any general content with the result of his term than I do.

※

In avoiding the appearance of evil, I am not sure but I have sometimes unnecessarily deprived myself and others of innocent enjoyment.

Fighting battles is like courting girls: those who make the most pretensions and are boldest usually win.

My policy is trust—peace, and to put aside the bayonet.

※

I am not liked as a president by the politicians in office, in the press, or in Congress. But I am confident to abide the judgment—the sober second thought—of the people.

The president of the United States of necessity owes his election to office to the suffrage and zealous labors of a political party the members of which cherish with ardor and regard as of essential importance the principles of their party organization; but he should strive to be always mindful of the fact that he serves his party best who serves his country best.

Let me assure my countrymen of the Southern States that it is my earnest desire to regard and promote their truest interest—the interests of the white and of the colored people both and equally—and to put forth my best efforts in behalf of a civil policy which will forever wipe out in our political affairs the color line and the distinction between North and South, to the end that we may have not merely a united North or a united South, but a united country.

In furtherance of the reform we seek, and in other important respects a change of great importance, I recommend an amendment to the Constitution prescribing a term of six years for the Presidential office and forbidding a reelection.

The capital of the nation should be something more than a mere political center. We should avail ourselves of all the opportunities which Providence has here placed at our command to promote the general intelligence of the people and increase the conditions most favorable to the success and perpetuity of our institutions.

It is the desire of the good people of the whole country that sectionalism as a factor in our politics should disappear.

❧

Let all our dealings with the Red Man be characterized by justice and good faith, and let there be the most liberal provision for his physical wants, for education in its widest sense, and for religious instruction and training.

❧

Only a few presidents have had the felicity to see their party stronger at the close of their terms than it was at the beginning. Only a few have left their country more prosperous than they found it.

JAMES A. GARFIELD

20TH PRESIDENT • MARCH–SEPTEMBER 1881
Born: November 19, 1831, in Orange, Ohio
Died: September 19, 1881, in Elberon, New Jersey

Wife: Lucretia Rudolph

Religion: Disciples of Christ

Education: Williams College

Other political offices held: Ohio State Senator, Member of U.S. House of Representatives, U.S. Senator

The second president to be assassinated, James A. Garfield was the last president who was born in a log cabin. The first left-handed president, Garfield would write Latin with one hand and Greek with the other. He was shot at the Washington railroad station by a mentally disturbed office-seeker and died eleven weeks later from blood poisoning.

We can not overestimate the fervent love of liberty, the intelligent courage, and the sum of common sense with which our fathers made the great experiment of self-government.

Fellow citizens, God reigns and the government at Washington still lives.

Justice and goodwill will outlast passion.

Under this Constitution the boundaries of freedom have been enlarged, the foundations of order and peace have been strengthened, and the growth of our people in all the better elements of national life has indicated the wisdom of the founders and given new hope to their descendants.

A pound of pluck is worth a ton of luck.

I am trying to do two things: dare to be a radical and not a fool, which is a matter of no small difficulty.

A nation is not worthy to be saved if, in the hour of its fate, it will not gather up all its jewels of manhood and life, and go down into the conflict, however bloody and doubtful, resolved on measureless ruin or complete success.

---

* *

Ideas control the world.

If you are not too large for the place you occupy, you are too small for it.

☙

The supremacy of the nation and its laws should be no longer a subject of debate. That discussion, which for half a century threatened the existence of the Union, was closed at last in the high court of war by a decree from which there is no appeal—that the Constitution and the laws made in pursuance thereof are and shall continue to be the supreme law of the land, binding alike upon the States and the people.

☙

A brave man is a man who dares to look the Devil in the face and tell him he is a Devil.

☙

If wrinkles must be written upon our brows, let them not be written upon the heart. The spirit should not grow old.

☙

Poverty is uncomfortable; but nine times out of ten the best thing that can happen to a young man is to be tossed overboard and compelled to sink or swim.

All free governments are managed by the combined wisdom and folly of the people.

*

The supreme trial of the Constitution came at last under the tremendous pressure of civil war. We ourselves are witnesses that the Union emerged from the blood and fire of that conflict purified and made stronger for all the beneficent purposes of good government.

*

The President is the last person in the world to know what the people really want and think.

*

The elevation of the Negro race from slavery to the full rights of citizenship is the most important political change we have known since the adoption of the Constitution of 1787. No thoughtful man can fail to appreciate its beneficent effect upon our institutions and people. It has freed us from the perpetual danger of war and dissolution. It has added immensely to the moral and industrial forces of our people. It has liberated the master as well as the slave from a relation which wronged and enfeebled both. It has surrendered to their own guardianship the manhood of more than 5,000,000 people, and has opened to each one of them a career of freedom and usefulness. It has given new inspiration to the power of self-help in both races by making labor more honorable to the one and more necessary to the other. The influence of this force will grow greater and bear richer fruit with the coming years.

CHESTER A. ARTHUR

21ST PRESIDENT • 1881–1885

Born: October 5, 1830, in Fairfield, Vermont
Died: November 18, 1886, in New York, New York

Wife: Ellen Lewis Herndon

Religion: Episcopalian

Education: Union College

Other political offices: Vice President

The son of an itinerant Baptist preacher, Chester A. Arthur was named president after Garfield's assassination. Arthur signed the Pendleton Act that created the modern civil service system, and the vice presidency was his first and only elected office. Known as "The Gentleman Boss," Arthur hired the most famous designer in New York, Louis Comfort Tiffany, to transform the White House into a showplace.

★ ★

I may be president of the United States, but my private life is nobody's damned business.

If it were not for the reporters, I would tell you the truth.

Good ballplayers make good citizens.

> # Men may die, but the fabrics of our free institutions remain unshaken.

No higher or more assuring proof could exist of the strength and permanence of popular government than the fact that though the chosen of the people be struck down, his constitutional successor is peacefully installed without shock or strain except the sorrow which mourns the bereavement.

Well, there doesn't seem to be anything else for an ex-president to do but go into the country and raise big pumpkins.

All personal consideration and political views must be merged in the national sorrow. I am an American among millions grieving for their wounded chief.

GROVER CLEVELAND

22ND PRESIDENT • 1885–1889
24TH PRESIDENT • 1893–1897
Born: March 18, 1837, in Caldwell, New Jersey
Died: June 24, 1908, in Princeton, New Jersey

Wife: Frances Folsom

Religion: Presbyterian

Education: No formal education

Other political offices: Sheriff of Erie County, New York; Mayor of
Buffalo, New York; Governor of New York

The only president to serve two nonconsecutive terms, Grover
Cleveland dedicated the Statue of Liberty and signed the Presidential Succession Act and the anti-polygamy act. He was the only president married in the White House, and the Baby Ruth candy bar was
named after his baby daughter, Ruth.

* *

What is the use of being elected or reelected, unless you stand for something?

❧

I mistake the American people if they favor the odious doctrine that there is no such thing as international morality; that there is one law for a strong nation and another for a weak one.

❧

Our duties are practical and call for industrious application, an intelligent perception of the claims of public office, and, above all, a firm determination, by united action, to secure to all the people of the land the full benefits of the best form of government ever vouchsafed to man. And let us not trust to human effort alone, but humbly acknowledging the power and goodness of Almighty God, who presides over the destiny of nations, and who has at all times been revealed in our country's history, let us invoke His aid and His blessings upon our labors.

❧

Fully impressed with the gravity of the duties that confront me and mindful of my weakness, I should be appalled if it were my lot to bear unaided the responsibilities which await me.

❧

I find also much comfort in remembering that my countrymen are just and generous and in the assurance that they will not condemn those who by sincere devotion to their service deserve their forbearance and approval.

★ ★

> A man is known by the company he keeps, and also by the company from which he is kept out.

I have considered the pension list of the republic a roll of honor.

ॐ

I have tried so hard to do right.

ॐ

The ship of democracy which has weathered all storms may sink through the mutiny of those aboard.

ॐ

I am honest and sincere in my desire to do well, but the question is whether I know enough to accomplish what I desire.

ॐ

When more of the people's sustenance is exacted through the form of taxation than is necessary to meet the just obligations of government and expenses of its economical administration, such exaction becomes ruthless extortion and a violation of the fundamental principles of free government.

Officeholders are the agents of the people, not their masters.

~

Loyalty to the principles upon which our Government rests positively demands that the equality before the law which it guarantees to every citizen should be justly and in good faith conceded in all parts of the land. The enjoyment of this right follows the badge of citizenship wherever found, and, unimpaired by race or color, it appeals for recognition to American manliness and fairness.

~

There is no calamity which a great nation can invite which equals that which follows a supine submission to wrong and injustice and the consequent loss of national self-respect and honor, beneath which are shielded and defended a people's safety and greatness.

~

He mocks the people who proposes that the government shall protect the rich and that they in turn will care for the laboring poor.

~

It is the responsibility of the citizens to support their government. It is not the responsibility of the government to support its citizens.

~

Every citizen owes to the country a vigilant watch and close scrutiny of its public servants and affairs and a reasonable estimate of their fidelity and usefulness.

In the presence of this vast assemblage of my countrymen I am about to supplement and seal by the oath which I shall take the manifestation of the will of a great and free people. In the exercise of their power and right of self-government they have committed to one of their fellow-citizens a supreme and sacred trust, and he here consecrates himself to their service.

❧

Your every voter, as surely as your chief magistrate, exercises a public trust.

❧

While every American citizen must contemplate with the utmost pride and enthusiasm the growth and expansion of our country, the sufficiency of our institutions to stand against the rudest shocks of violence, the wonderful thrift and enterprise of our people, and the demonstrated superiority of our free government, it behooves us to constantly watch for every symptom of insidious infirmity that threatens our national vigor.

❧

A truly American sentiment recognizes the dignity of labor and the fact that honor lies in honest toil.

❧

Communism is a hateful thing, and a menace to peace and organized government.

❧

Minds do not act together in public; they simply stick together; and when their private activities are resumed, they fly apart again.

BENJAMIN HARRISON

23RD PRESIDENT • 1889–1893

Born: August 20, 1833, in North Bend, Ohio
Died: March 13, 1901, in Indianapolis, Indiana

Wives: Caroline Lavinia Scott; Mary Scott Lord

Religion: Presbyterian

Education: Miami University, Ohio

Other political offices: U.S. Senator

The grandson of William Henry Harrison, the ninth U.S. president, Benjamin Harrison was born to a life of wealth and privilege. During his term of office, Harrison successfully lobbied for the Sherman Silver Act, which required that silver be used in federal coinage. Harrison advocated conserving forest reserves and supported the Sherman Antitrust Act, which attempted to limit the power of America's giant corporations. He named former slave Frederick Douglass as ambassador to Haiti.

* *

Let those who would die for the flag on the field of battle give a better proof of their patriotism and a higher glory to their country by promoting fraternity and justice.

Where the children of rich and poor mingle together on the playground and in the schoolroom, there is produced a unity of feeling and a popular love for public institutions that can be brought about in no other way.

The patriotism of the people, which no longer found afield of exercise in war, was energetically directed to the duty of equipping the young Republic for the defense of its independence by making its people self-dependent.

We shall neither fail to respect the flag of any friendly nation or the just rights of its citizens, nor to exact the like treatment for our own. Calmness, justice, and consideration should characterize our diplomacy.

No other people have a government more worthy of their respect and love or a land so magnificent in extent, so pleasant to look upon, and so full of generous suggestion to enterprise and labor. God has placed upon our head a diadem and has laid at our feet power and wealth beyond definition or calculation. But we must not forget that we take these gifts upon the condition that justice and mercy shall hold the reins of power and that the upward avenues of hope shall be free to all the people.

I knew that my staying up would not change the election result if I were defeated, while if elected I had a hard day ahead of me. So I thought a night's rest was best in any event.

§

We shall find unalloyed pleasure in the revelation which our next census will make of the swift development of the great resources of some of the States. Each State will bring its generous contribution to the great aggregate of the nation's increase. And when the harvests from the fields, the cattle from the hills, and the ores of the earth shall have been weighed, counted, and valued, we will turn from them all to crown with the highest honor the State that has most promoted education, virtue, justice, and patriotism among its people.

§

We Americans have no commission from God to police the world.

§

The Yankee intermingles with the Illinoisan, the Hoosier with the Sucker, and the people of the South with them all and it is this comingling which gives that unity which marks the American nation.

§

What questions are we to grapple with? What unfinished work remains to be done? It seems to me that the work that is unfinished is to make that constitutional grant of citizenship, the franchise to the colored men of the South, a practical and living reality.

> **I** believe also in the American opportunity which puts the starry sky above every boy's head, and sets his foot upon a ladder which he may climb until his strength gives out.

I said to one of the first delegations that visited me that this was a contest of great principles; that it would be fought out upon the high plains of truth, and not in the swamps of slander and defamation. Those who will encamp their army in the swamp will abandon the victory to the army that is on the heights.

I pity the man who wants a coat so cheap that the man or woman who produces the cloth will starve in the process.

Two presidents or three, with equal powers, would as surely bring disaster as three generals of equal rank and command in a single army. I do not doubt that this sense of single and personal responsibility to the people has strongly held our presidents to a good conscience, and to a high discharge of their duties.

The manner by which women are treated is a good criterion to judge the true state of society. If we know but this one feature in a character of a nation, we may easily judge the rest, for as society advances, the true character of women is discovered.

*

There is no constitutional or legal requirement that the President shall take the oath of office in the presence of the people, but there is so manifest an appropriateness in the public induction to office of the chief executive officer of the nation that from the beginning of the Government the people, to whose service the official oath consecrates the officer, have been called to witness the solemn ceremonial. The oath taken in the presence of the people becomes a mutual covenant. The officer covenants to serve the whole body of the people by a faithful execution of the laws, so that they may be the unfailing defense and security of those who respect and observe them, and that neither wealth, station, nor the power of combinations shall be able to evade their just penalties or to wrest them from a beneficent public purpose to serve the ends of cruelty or selfishness.

WILLIAM McKINLEY

25TH PRESIDENT • 1897–1901
Born: January 29, 1843, in Niles, Ohio
Died: September 14, 1901 in Buffalo, New York

Wife: Ida Saxon

Religion: Methodist

Education: Attended Allegheny College

Other political offices: Member of U.S. House of Representatives, Governor of Ohio

William McKinley defeated William Jennings Bryan in two elections for the presidency. McKinley's first term in office was dominated by the Spanish-American War, declared after the sinking of the U.S. battleship *Maine* in Cuba's Havana harbor. He was the third president to be assassinated.

That's all a man can hope for during his lifetime—to set an example—and when he is dead, to be an inspiration for history.

*

Unlike any other nation, here the people rule, and their will is the supreme law. It is sometimes sneeringly said by those who do not like free government, that here we count heads. True, heads are counted, but brains also.

*

We want no war of conquest. . . . War should never be entered upon until every agency of peace has failed.

*

I have never been in doubt since I was old enough to think intelligently that I would someday be made president.

*

I have already transmitted to Congress the report of the naval court of inquiry on the destruction of the battleship *Maine* in the harbor of Havana during the night of the fifteenth of February. The destruction of that noble vessel has filled the national heart with inexpressible horror. Two hundred and fifty-eight brave sailors and marines and two officers of our Navy, reposing in the fancied security of a friendly harbor, have been hurled to death, grief and want brought to their homes and sorrow to the nation.

*

We need Hawaii just as much and a good deal more than we did California. It is manifest Destiny.

> **I**lliteracy must be banished from the land if we shall attain that high destiny as the foremost of the enlightened nations of the world which, under Providence, we ought to achieve.

Business life, whether among ourselves or with other people, is ever a sharp struggle for success. It will be none the less so in the future. Without competition we would be clinging to the clumsy antiquated processes of farming and manufacture and the methods of business of long ago, and the twentieth would be no further advanced than the eighteenth century.

It is inspiring, too, to remember that no great emergency in the one hundred and eight years of our eventful national life has ever arisen that has not been met with wisdom and courage by the American people, with fidelity to their best interests and highest destiny, and to the honor of the American name. These years of glorious history have exalted mankind and advanced the cause of freedom throughout the world, and immeasurably strengthened the precious free institutions which we enjoy. The people love and will sustain these institutions.

The American people, entrenched in freedom at home, take their love for it with them wherever they go, and they reject as mistaken and unworthy the doctrine that we lose our own liberties by securing the enduring foundations of liberty to others. Our institutions will not deteriorate by extension, and our sense of justice will not abate under tropic suns in distant seas.

In conclusion, I congratulate the country upon the fraternal spirit of the people and the manifestations of good will everywhere so apparent. The recent election not only most fortunately demonstrated the obliteration of sectional or geographical lines, but to some extent also the prejudices which for years have distracted our councils and marred our true greatness as a nation. The triumph of the people, whose verdict is carried into effect today, is not the triumph of one section, nor wholly of one party, but of all sections and all the people. The North and the South no longer divide on the old lines, but upon principles and policies; and in this fact surely every lover of the country can find cause for true felicitation. Let us rejoice in and cultivate this spirit; it is ennobling and will be both a gain and a blessing to our beloved country. It will be my constant aim to do nothing, and permit nothing to be done, that will arrest or disturb this growing sentiment of unity and cooperation, this revival of esteem and affiliation which now animates so many thousands in both the old antagonistic sections, but I shall cheerfully do everything possible to promote and increase it.

One of the lessons taught by the late election, which all can rejoice in, is that the citizens of the United States are both law-respecting and law-abiding people, not easily swerved from the path of patriotism and honor.

Strong hearts and helpful hands are needed, and, fortunately, we have them in every part of our beloved country. We are reunited. Sectionalism has disappeared. Division on public questions can no longer be traced by the war maps of 1861.

The faith of the fathers was a mighty force in its creation, and the faith of their descendants has wrought its progress and furnished its defenders.

Lynchings must not be tolerated in a great and civilized country like the United States; courts, not mobs, must execute the penalties of the law. The preservation of public order, the right of discussion, the integrity of courts, and the orderly administration of justice must continue forever the rock of safety upon which our Government securely rests.

Force will not be needed or used when those who make war against us shall make it no more. May it end without further bloodshed, and there be ushered in the reign of peace to be made permanent by a government of liberty under law!

THEODORE ROOSEVELT

26TH PRESIDENT • 1901–1909

Born: October 27, 1858, in New York, New York
Died: January 6, 1919, in Oyster Bay, New York

Wives: Alice Hathaway Lee; Edith Kermit Carow

Religion: Dutch Reformed

Education: Harvard College

Other political offices: Member of New York State Assembly, Assistant Secretary of the Navy, Governor of New York, Vice President

The only president born in New York City, Theodore Roosevelt was the commander of the Rough Riders cavalry regiment during the Spanish-American War. At forty-two, Roosevelt became the youngest president upon assuming office following McKinley's assassination. During his terms, Roosevelt began construction of the Panama Canal. He was awarded the Nobel Peace Prize after mediating the end of the Russo-Japanese War.

★ ★

Actions speak louder than words.

✍

No man is justified in doing evil on the ground of expediency.

✍

Far and away the best prize that life has to offer is the chance to work hard at work worth doing.

✍

The best executive is one who has sense enough to pick good people to do what he wants done, and self-restraint enough to keep from meddling with them while they do it.

✍

Perhaps the most characteristic educational movement of the past fifty years is that which has created the modern public library and developed it into broad and active service. There are now over five thousand public libraries in the United States, the product of this period. In addition to accumulating material, they are also striving by organization, by improvement in method, and by cooperation, to give greater efficiency to the material they hold, to make it more widely useful, and by avoidance of unnecessary duplication in process to reduce the cost of its administration.

✍

People ask the difference in a leader and a boss. The leader leads and the boss drives.

The worst fear is the fear of living.

To educate a man in mind and not in morals is to educate a menace to society.

There is only one quality worse than hardness of the heart and that is softness of head.

I have often been afraid, but I wouldn't give into it. I made myself act as though I was not afraid, and gradually my fear disappeared.

In any moment of decision, the best thing you can do is the right thing, the next best thing is the wrong thing. The worst thing you can do is nothing.

Speak softly and carry a big stick; you will go far.

The most important single ingredient in the formula of success is knowing how to get along with people.

You never have trouble if you are prepared for it.

We cannot do great deeds unless we are willing to do the small things that make up the sum of greatness.

> Life brings sorrows and joys alike. It is what a man does with them—not what they do to him—that is the true test of his mettle.

To sit home, read one's favorite paper, and scoff at the misdeeds of the men who do things is easy, but it is markedly ineffective. It is what evil men count upon the good men's doing.

❧

Measure iniquity by the heart, whether a man's purse be full or empty, partly full or partly empty. If the man is a decent man, whether well off or not well off, stand by him; if he is not a decent man stand against him, whether he be rich or poor.

❧

We have become a great nation, forced by the fact of its greatness into relations with the other nations of the earth, and we must behave as beseems a people with such responsibilities. Toward all other nations, large and small, our attitude must be one of cordial and sincere friendship. We must show not only in our words, but in our deeds, that we are earnestly desirous of securing their good will by acting toward them in a spirit of just and generous recognition of all their rights.

Nine-tenths of wisdom consists in being wise in time.

> Whenever you are asked if you can do a job, tell 'em, "Certainly, I can!" Then get busy and find out how to do it.

A man who is good enough to shed his blood for his country is good enough to be given a square deal, because he is entitled to no more and should receive no less.

*

Order without liberty and liberty without order are equally destructive.

*

It is well indeed for our land that we of this generation have learned to think nationally.

*

Far better it is to dare mighty things, to win glorious triumphs, even though checkered by failure, than to take rank with those poor spirits who neither enjoy much nor suffer much, because they live in the gray twilight that knows not victory nor defeat.

★ ★

A stream cannot rise larger than its source.

❧

I wish to preach, not the doctrine of ignoble ease, but the doctrine of the strenuous life.

❧

No man is above the law and no man is below it; nor do we ask any man's permission when we require him to obey it. Obedience to the law is demanded as a right; not asked as a favor.

❧

The only man who makes no mistake is the man who does nothing.

❧

To waste, to destroy, our natural resources, to skin and exhaust the land instead of using it so as to increase its usefulness, will result in undermining in the days of our children the very prosperity which we ought by right to hand down to them amplified and developed.

❧

Americanism is a question of principle, of purpose, of idealism, of character; it is not a matter of birthplace or creed or line of descent.

❧

No other President ever enjoyed the Presidency as I did.

❧

I feel as fit as a bull moose.

It is hard to fail, but it is worse never to have tried to succeed.

※

A great debt is owing from the public to the men of the army and navy. They should be so treated as to enable them to reach the highest point of efficiency, so that they may be able to respond instantly to any demand made upon them to sustain the interests of the nation and the honor of the flag. The individual American enlisted man is probably on the whole a more formidable fighting man than the regular of any other army. Every consideration should be shown him, and in return the highest standard of usefulness should be exacted from him. It is well worthwhile for the Congress to consider whether the pay of enlisted men upon second and subsequent enlistments should not be increased to correspond with the increased value of the veteran soldier.

※

There is no room in this country for hyphenated Americanism.

※

Your attitude about who you are and what you have is a very little thing that makes a very big difference.

※

Of course the all-important thing to keep in mind is that if we have not both strength and virtue we shall fail.

※

Rhetoric is a poor substitute for action.

I have never won anything without hard labor and the exercise of my good judgment and careful planning and working long in advance.

≈

Progress has brought us both unbounded opportunities and unbridled difficulties. Thus the measure of our civilization will not be that we have done much, but what we have done with that much.

≈

The most successful politician says what everybody is thinking most often and in the loudest voice.

≈

There has never yet been a man in our history who led a life of ease whose name is worth remembering.

≈

To discriminate against a thoroughly upright citizen because he belongs to some particular church, or because, like Abraham Lincoln, he has not avowed his allegiance to any church, is an outrage against that liberty of conscience which is one of the foundations of American life.

≈

When you play, play hard. When you work, don't play at all.

≈

Unless a man is honest we have no right to keep him in public life; it matters not how brilliant his capacity.

Indeed, in the old acceptation of the word, virtue included strength and courage, for the clear-sighted men at the dawn of our era knew that the passive virtues could not by themselves avail, that wisdom without courage would sink into mere cunning, and courage without morality into ruthless, lawless, self-destructive ferocity.

The first requisite of a good citizen in this Republic of ours is that he shall be able and willing to pull his own weight.

If I must choose between righteousness and peace, I choose righteousness.

※

The hardest lessons to learn are those that are the most obvious.

※

The country needs and, unless I mistake its temper, the country demands bold, persistent experimentation. It is common sense to take a method and try it; if it fails, admit it frankly and try another. But above all, try something.

Honesty is . . . an absolute prerequisite to efficient service to the public.

❦

A square deal for every man; that is the only safe motto for the United States.

❦

If an American is to amount to anything he must rely upon himself, and not upon the State; he must take pride in his own work, instead of sitting idle to envy the luck of others. He must face life with resolute courage, win victory if he can, and accept defeat if he must, without seeking to place on his fellow man a responsibility which is not theirs.

❦

A vote is like a rifle: its usefulness depends upon the character of the user.

❦

Our country offers the most wonderful example of democratic government on a giant scale that the world has ever seen; and the peoples of the world are watching to see whether we succeed or fail.

❦

Be honest, and remember that honesty counts for nothing unless back of it lie courage and efficiency.

❦

Let us speak courteously, deal fairly, and keep ourselves armed and ready.

From the largest to the smallest, happiness and usefulness are largely found in the same souls, and the joy of life is won in the deepest and truest sense only by those who have not shirked life's burdens.

❧

Unless a man is master of his soul, all other kinds of mastery amount to little.

❧

Nothing in the world is worth having or worth doing unless it means effort, pain, difficulty. . . . I have never in my life envied a human being who led an easy life. I have envied a great many people who led difficult lives and lived them well.

❧

The American people are slow to wrath, but when their wrath is once kindled it burns like a consuming flame.

❧

It is not what we have that will make us a great nation; it is the way in which we use it.

❧

From the standpoint of the nation, and from the broader standpoint of mankind, scholarship is of worth chiefly when it is productive, when the scholar not merely receives or acquires, but gives.

❧

We are face to face with our destiny and we must meet it with a high and resolute courage.

★ ★

I have only a second rate brain, but I think I have a capacity for action.

Life is not easy, and least of all is it easy for either the man or the nation that aspires to great deeds.

Envy is as evil a thing as arrogance.

༄

The one thing I want to leave my children is an honorable name.

༄

I keep my good health by having a very bad temper, kept under good control.

༄

This country will not be a permanent good place for any of us to live in unless we make it a reasonably good place for all of us to live in.

༄

We have got but one life here. It pays, no matter what comes after it, to try and do things, to accomplish things in this life and not merely to have a soft and pleasant time.

We need the iron qualities that go with true manhood. We need the positive virtues of resolution, of courage, of indomitable will, of power to do without shrinking the rough work that must always be done.

❦

No prosperity and no glory can save a nation that is rotten at heart.

❦

There is not in all America a more dangerous trait than the deification of mere smartness unaccompanied by any sense of moral responsibility.

❦

All that the law can do is to shape things so that no injustice shall be done by one to the other, and that each man shall be given the first chance to show the stuff that is in him.

❦

More and more, as it becomes necessary to preserve the game, let us hope that the camera will largely supplant the rifle.

❦

Our country has been populated by pioneers, and therefore it has more energy, more enterprise, more expansive power than any other in the whole world.

❦

The unforgivable crime is soft hitting. Do not hit at all if it can be avoided; but never hit softly.

We are the heirs of the ages.

Bodily vigor is good, and vigor of intellect is even better, but far above is character.

Let the watchwords of all our people be the old familiar watchwords of honesty, decency, fair dealing and common sense.

A man who never has gone to school may steal from a freight car, but if he has a university education, he may steal from the whole railroad.

Do what you can, with what you have, where you are.

Courtesy is as much a mark of a gentleman as courage.

We in our turn have an assured confidence that we shall be able to leave this heritage unwasted and enlarged to our children and our children's children. To do so we must show, not merely in great crises, but in the everyday affairs of life, the qualities of practical intelligence, of courage, of hardihood, and endurance, and above all the power of devotion to a lofty ideal, which made great the men who founded this Republic in the days of Washington, which made great the men who preserved this Republic in the days of Abraham Lincoln.

Anarchy is a crime against the whole human race; and all mankind should band against the anarchist. His crime should be made an offense against the law of nations, like piracy and that form of man-stealing known as the slave trade, for it is of far blacker infamy than either.

✺

We can afford to differ on the currency, the tariff and foreign policy, but we cannot afford to differ on the question of honesty if we expect our republic permanently to endure.

✺

It is true of the Nation, as of the individual, that the greatest doer must also be the great dreamer.

✺

Be practical as well as generous in your ideals. Keep your eyes on the stars, but remember to keep your feet on the ground.

✺

Success, the real success, does not depend upon the position you hold but upon how you carry yourself in that position.

✺

It is always better to be an original than an imitation.

✺

No nation has greater resources than ours, and I think it can be truthfully said that the citizens of no nation possess greater energy and industrial ability.

WILLIAM H. TAFT

27TH PRESIDENT • 1909–1913
Born: September 15, 1857, in Cincinnati, Ohio
Died: March 8, 1930, in Washington, D.C.

Wife: Helen Herron

Religion: Unitarian

Education: Yale College, Cincinnati Law School

Other political offices: Judge in Ohio Superior Court, U.S. Solicitor General, U.S. Circuit Court Judge, Governor of the Philippines, Secretary of War, Chief Justice of the U.S. Supreme Court

William H. Taft began the tradition of throwing out the first pitch of the major league baseball season. He was credited for bringing eighty antitrust suits that, among other things, broke up Standard Oil and American Tobacco. After his term as president, Taft became chief justice of the U.S. Supreme Court.

A government is for the benefit of the people.

❧

The diplomacy of the present administration has
sought to respond to modern ideas of commercial
intercourse. This policy has been characterized as
substituting dollars for bullets. It is one that appeals
alike to idealistic humanitarian sentiments, to the
dictates of sound policy and strategy, and to legitimate
commercial aims.

❧

The Negroes are now Americans . . . this is their only
country and their only flag. They have shown
themselves anxious to live for it and to die for it.

❧

Socialism proposes no adequate substitute for the
motive of enlightened selfishness that today is at the
basis of all human labor and effort, enterprise and new
activity.

❧

Anti-Semitism is a noxious weed that should be cut
out. It has no place in America.

❧

Next to the right of liberty, the right of property is the
most important individual right guaranteed by the
Constitution and the one which, united with that of
personal liberty, has contributed more to the growth of
civilization than any other institution established by
the human race.

★ ★

Anyone who has taken the oath I have just taken must feel a heavy weight of responsibility. If not, he has no conception of the powers and duties of the office upon which he is about to enter, or he is lacking in a proper sense of the obligation which the oath imposes.

> # Our international policy is always to promote peace.

Personally, I have not the slightest race prejudice or feeling, and recognition of its existence only awakens in my heart a deeper sympathy for those who have to bear it or suffer from it, and I question the wisdom of a policy which is likely to increase it.

I look forward with hope to increasing the already good feeling between the South and the other sections of the country. My chief purpose is not to effect a change in the electoral vote of the Southern States. That is a secondary consideration. What I look forward to is an increase in the tolerance of political views of all kinds and their advocacy throughout the South, and the existence of a respectable political opposition in every State; even more than this, to an increased feeling on the part of all the people in the South that this Government is their Government, and that its officers in their States are their officers.

We should have an army so organized and so officered as to be capable in time of emergency, in cooperation with the national militia and under the provisions of a proper national volunteer law, rapidly to expand into a force sufficient to resist all probable invasion from abroad and to furnish a respectable expeditionary force if necessary in the maintenance of our traditional American policy which bears the name of President Monroe.

The construction of the Lincoln Memorial and of a memorial bridge from the base of the Washington Monument to Arlington would be an appropriate and symbolic expression of the union of the North and the South at the Capital of the Nation. I urge upon Congress the appointment of a commission to undertake these national improvements, and to submit a plan for their execution; and when the plan has been submitted and approved, and the work carried out, Washington will really become what it ought to be—the most beautiful city in the world.

WOODROW WILSON

28TH PRESIDENT • 1913–1921

Born: December 28, 1856, in Staunton, Virginia
Died: February 2, 1924, in Washington, D.C.

Wives: Ellen Louise Axon; Edith Bulling Gait

Religion: Presbyterian

Education: College of New Jersey

Other political offices: Governor of New Jersey

The only president who earned a Ph.D., Woodrow Wilson taught history and politics at Bryn Mawr, Wesleyan, and Princeton before becoming president of Princeton in 1902. Wilson pushed through the Federal Reserve Act of 1913, which created the strong federal system that today still provides the framework for regulating the nation's banks, credit, and money supply. He also instituted daylight savings time to save fuel and oversaw America's entry into World War I. The Nineteenth Amendment, giving women the right to vote, was ratified during his term.

If you want to make enemies, try to change something.

America is not anything if it consists of each of us. It is something only if it consists of all of us.

Friendship is the only cement that will hold the world together.

The nation's honor is dearer than the nation's comfort; yes, than the nation's life itself.

The sum of the whole matter is this, that our civilization cannot survive materially unless it be redeemed spiritually.

Congress in session is Congress on public exhibition, whilst Congress in its committee rooms is Congress at work.

We live in an age disturbed, confused, bewildered, afraid of its own forces, in search not merely of its road but even of its direction. There are many voices of counsel, but few voices of vision; there is much excitement and feverish activity, but little concert of thoughtful purpose. We are distressed by our own ungoverned, undirected energies and do many things, but nothing long. It is our duty to find ourselves.

The state exists for the sake of society, not society for the sake of the state.

❧

Sometimes people call me an idealist. Well, that is the way I know I am an American. America, my fellow citizens—I do not say it in disparagement of any other great people—America is the only idealistic nation in the world.

❧

One cool judgment is worth a thousand hasty counsels. The thing to be supplied is light, not heat.

❧

The history of liberty is a history of resistance. The history of liberty is a history of the limitation of governmental power, not the increase of it.

❧

I would rather belong to a poor nation that was free than to a rich nation that had ceased to be in love with liberty. But we shall not be poor if we love liberty, because the nation that loves liberty truly sets every man free to do his best and be his best, and that means the release of all the splendid energies of a great people who think for themselves. A nation of employees cannot be free any more than a nation of employers can be.

❧

Only a peace between equals can last. Only a peace the very principle of which is equality and a common participation in a common benefit.

★ ★

The world must be made safe for democracy.

We grow great by dreams. All big men are dreamers.

჻

You cannot be friends upon any other terms than upon the terms of equality.

჻

It is a fearful thing to lead this great peaceful people into war, into the most terrible and disastrous of all wars, civilization itself seeming to be in the balance. But the right is more precious than peace, and we shall fight for the things which we have always carried nearest our hearts, for democracy, for the right of those who submit to authority to have a voice in their own governments, for the rights and liberties of small nations, for a universal dominion of right by such a concert of free peoples as shall bring peace and safety to all nations and make the world itself at last free. To such a task we dedicate our lives and our fortunes, everything that we are and everything that we have, with the pride of those who know that the day has come when America is privileged to spend her blood and her might for the principles that gave her birth and happiness and the peace which she has treasured. God helping her, she can do no other.

Loyalty means nothing unless it has at its heart the absolute principle of self-sacrifice.

❧

While we speak of the preparation of the nation to make sure of her security and her effective power, we must not fall into the patent error of supposing that her real strength comes from armaments and mere safeguards of written law. It comes, of course, from her people, their energy, their success in their undertakings, their free opportunity to use the natural resources of our great homeland and of the lands outside our continental borders which look to us for protection, for encouragement, and for assistance in their development; from the organization and freedom of our economic life.

❧

There is a price which is too great to pay for peace, and that price can be put in one word. One cannot pay the price of self-respect.

❧

There must be, not a balance of power, but a community of power; not organized rivalries, but an organized peace.

❧

When I give a man an office, I watch him carefully to see whether he is swelling or growing.

❧

All the extraordinary men I have known were extraordinary in their own estimation.

Generally young men are regarded as radicals. This is
a popular misconception. The most conservative
persons I ever met are college undergraduates. The
radicals are the men past middle life.

*

I would rather lose in a cause that will some day win,
than win in a cause that will some day lose!

*

A man who thinks of himself as belonging to a
particular national group in America has not yet
become an American.

*

I close, as I began, by reminding you of the great tasks
and duties of peace which challenge our best powers
and invite us to build what will last, the tasks to which
we can address ourselves now and at all times with free-
hearted zest and with all the finest gifts of constructive
wisdom we possess. To develop our life and our
resources; to supply our own people, and the people of
the world as their need arises, from the abundant
plenty of our fields and our marts of trade, to enrich
the commerce of our own States and of the world with
the products of our mines, our farms, and our
factories, with the creations of our thought and the
fruits of our character, this is what will hold our
attention and our enthusiasm steadily, now and in the
years to come, as we strive to show in our life as a
nation what liberty and the inspirations of an
emancipated spirit may do for men and for societies,
for individuals, for states, and for mankind.

I would never read a book if it were possible for me to talk half an hour with the man who wrote it.

⁂

The wisest thing to do with a fool is to encourage him to hire a hall and discourse to his fellow citizens. Nothing chills nonsense like exposure to air.

⁂

I have always been among those who believed that the greatest freedom of speech was the greatest safety, because if a man is a fool, the best thing to do is to encourage him to advertise the fact by speaking.

⁂

I have spoken plainly because this seems to me the time when it is most necessary to speak plainly, in order that all the world may know that, even in the heat and ardor of the struggle and when our whole thought is of carrying the war through to its end, we have not forgotten any ideal or principle for which the name of America has been held in honor among the nations and for which it has been our glory to contend in the great generations that went before us. A supreme moment of history has come. The eyes of the people have been opened and they see. The hand of God is laid upon the nations. He will show them favor, I devoutly believe, only if they rise to the clear heights of His justice and mercy.

⁂

There is no cause half so sacred as the cause of a people. There is no idea so uplifting as the idea of the service of humanity.

> The man who is swimming against the stream knows the strength of it.

I am all kinds of a democrat, so far as I can discover—but the root of the whole business is this, that I believe in the patriotism and energy and initiative of the average man.

A conservative is a man who sits and thinks, mostly thinks.

The use of a university is to make young gentleman as unlike their fathers as possible.

I believe in democracy because it releases the energies of every human being.

The Americans who went to Europe to die are a unique breed. Never before have men crossed the seas to a foreign land to fight for a cause which they did not pretend was peculiarly their own, which they knew was the cause of humanity and mankind. These Americans gave the greatest of all gifts, the gift of life and the gift of spirit.

In the last analysis, my fellow countrymen, as we in America would be the first to claim, a people are responsible for the acts of their government.

❧

Character is a by-product; it is produced in the great manufacture of daily duty.

❧

America is the place where you cannot kill your government by killing the men who conduct it.

❧

The firm basis of government is justice, not pity.

❧

In America there is but one way by which great reforms can be accomplished and the relief sought by classes obtained, and that is through the orderly processes of representative government.

❧

Nowhere else in the world have noble men and women exhibited in more striking forms the beauty and the energy of sympathy and helpfulness and counsel in their efforts to rectify wrong, alleviate suffering, and set the weak in the way of strength and hope. We have built up, moreover, a great system of government, which has stood through a long age as in many respects a model for those who seek to set liberty upon foundations that will endure against fortuitous change, against storm and accident. Our life contains every great thing, and contains it in rich abundance.

The first duty of law is to keep sound the society it serves.

❧

The feelings with which we face this new age of right and opportunity sweep across our heartstrings like some air out of God's own presence, where justice and mercy are reconciled and the judge and the brother are one.

❧

I summon all honest men, all patriotic, all forward-looking men, to my side. God helping me, I will not fail them, if they will but counsel and sustain me!

❧

Never murder a man who is committing suicide.

❧

The shadows that now lie dark upon our path will soon be dispelled, and we shall walk with the light all about us if we be but true to ourselves—to ourselves as we have wished to be known in the counsels of the world and in the thought of all those who love liberty and justice and the right exalted.

❧

As some of the injuries done us have become intolerable, we have still been clear that we wished nothing for ourselves that we were not ready to demand for all mankind—fair dealing, justice, the freedom to live and to be at ease against organized wrong.

It is not men that interest or disturb me primarily; it is ideas. Ideas live; men die.

There is no such a thing as a man being too proud to fight.

You catch, with me, the voices of humanity that are in the air. They grow daily more audible, more articulate, more persuasive, and they come from the hearts of men everywhere.

For what we are seeking now, what in my mind is the single thought of this message, is national efficiency and security. We serve a great nation. We should serve it in the spirit of its peculiar genius. It is the genius of common men for self-government, industry, justice, liberty, and peace. We should see to it that it lacks no instrument, no facility or vigor of law, to make it sufficient to play its part with energy, safety, and assured success. In this we are not partisans but heralds and prophets of a new age.

There is no indispensable man.

✣

The success of a party means little except when the Nation is using that party for a large and definite purpose.

✣

I pray God I may be given the wisdom and the prudence to do my duty in the true spirit of this great people. I am their servant and can succeed only as they sustain and guide me by their confidence and their counsel. The thing I shall count upon, the thing without which neither counsel nor action will avail, is the unity of America—an America united in feeling, in purpose and in its vision of duty, of opportunity and of service.

✣

Every people has a right to choose the sovereignty under which they shall live.

✣

What we all thank God for with deepest gratitude is that our men went in force into the line of battle just at the critical moment when the whole fate of the whole world seemed to hang in the balance and threw their fresh strength into the ranks of freedom in time to turn the whole tide and sweep the fateful struggle, turn it once and for all, so that thenceforth it was back, back, back for their enemies, always back, never again forward! After that it was only a scant four months before the commanders of the Central Empires knew themselves beaten; and now their very empires are in liquidation!

WARREN G. HARDING

29TH PRESIDENT • 1921–1923

Born: November 2, 1865, in Corsica, Ohio
Died: August 2, 1923, in San Francisco, California

Wife: Florence King De Wolfe

Religion: Baptist

Education: Ohio Central College

Other political offices: Ohio State Senator, Lieutenant Governor of Ohio, U.S. Senator

The first newspaper publisher to be elected president, Warren G. Harding was also the first president to own a radio and the first to speak over the radio airwaves. Though he was not involved, members of his administration were implicated in the Teapot Dome scandals, which centered around the lease of U.S. oil reserves. He died of a stroke during a visit to San Francisco.

We mean to have less of Government in business and more business in Government.

*

In the great fulfillment we must have a citizenship less concerned about what the government can do for it and more anxious about what it can do for the nation.

*

America's present need is not heroics, but healing; not nostrums but normalcy; not revolution, but restoration.

*

Today, better than ever before, we know the aspirations of humankind, and share them. We have come to a new realization of our place in the world and a new appraisal of our Nation by the world. The unselfishness of these United States is a thing proven; our devotion to peace for ourselves and for the world is well established; our concern for preserved civilization has had its impassioned and heroic expression.

*

Our most dangerous tendency is to expect too much of government, and at the same time do for it too little.

*

Government after all is a very simple thing.

*

Ours is a constitutional freedom where the popular will is the law supreme and minorities are sacredly protected.

I don't know much about Americanism, but it's a damn good word with which to carry an election.

> # Service is the supreme commitment of life.

We ought to find a way to guard against the perils and penalties of unemployment. We want an America of homes, illumined with hope and happiness, where mothers, freed from the necessity for long hours of toil beyond their own doors, may preside as befits the hearthstone of American citizenship. We want the cradle of American childhood rocked under conditions so wholesome and so hopeful that no blight may touch it in its development, and we want to provide that no selfish interest, no material necessity, no lack of opportunity shall prevent the gaining of that education so essential to best citizenship.

஺

Let the black man vote when he is fit to vote, prohibit the white man voting when he is unfit to vote.

஺

I love to meet people. It is the most pleasant thing I do; it is really the only fun I have. It does not tax me, and it seems to be a very great pleasure to them.

When one surveys the world about him after the great storm, noting the marks of destruction and yet rejoicing in the ruggedness of the things which withstood it, if he is an American he breathes the clarified atmosphere with a strange mingling of regret and new hope. We have seen a world passion spend its fury, but we contemplate our Republic unshaken, and hold our civilization secure. Liberty—liberty within the law—and civilization are inseparable, and though both were threatened we find them now secure; and there comes to Americans the profound assurance that our representative government is the highest expression and surest guaranty of both.

*

I have no trouble with my enemies. I can take care of my enemies all right. But my damn friends. They're the ones that keep me walking the floor at nights.

*

With the nation-wide induction of womanhood into our political life, we may count upon her intuitions, her refinements, her intelligence, and her influence to exalt the social order. We count upon her exercise of the full privileges and the performance of the duties of citizenship to speed the attainment of the highest state.

*

If I felt that there is to be sole responsibility in the Executive for the America of tomorrow I should shrink from the burden. But here are a hundred millions, with common concern and shared responsibility, answerable to God and country. The Republic summons them to their duty, and I invite co-operation.

In the beginning the Old World scoffed at our experiment; today our foundations of political and social belief stand unshaken, a precious inheritance to ourselves, an inspiring example of freedom and civilization to all mankind.

❧

Our eyes never will be blind to a developing menace, our ears never deaf to the call of civilization. We recognize the new order in the world, with the closer contacts which progress has wrought. We sense the call of the human heart for fellowship, fraternity, and cooperation. We crave friendship and harbor no hate.

❧

America is ready to encourage, eager to initiate, anxious to participate in any seemly program likely to lessen the probability of war, and promote that brotherhood of mankind which must be God's highest conception of human relationship.

❧

A regret for the mistakes of yesterday must not, however, blind us to the tasks of today.

❧

The forward course of the business cycle is unmistakable. Peoples are turning from destruction to production. Industry has sensed the changed order and our own people are turning to resume their normal, onward way. The call is for productive America to go on.

CALVIN COOLIDGE

30TH PRESIDENT • 1923–1929

Born: July 4, 1872, in Plymouth, Vermont
Died: January 5, 1933, in Northampton, Massachusetts

Wife: Grace Ann Goodhue

Religion: Congregationalist

Education: Amherst College

Other political offices: Northampton City Councilman, City
 Solicitor, Clerk of Courts, Member of Massachusetts
 Legislature, Mayor of Northampton, Lieutenant Governor of
 Massachusetts, Governor of Massachusetts, Vice President

Calvin Coolidge assumed office when President Harding died, and
was then elected for a full term. He rose to national prominence
when he used the militia to end the Boston police strike, and was
credited for reducing the national debt and lowering taxes. He also
introduced pro-business policies that encouraged stock-market spec-
ulation, which eventually led to the economic collapse of 1929.

The right thing to do never requires any subterfuge; it is always simple and direct.

Nothing in this world can take the place of persistence. Talent will not; nothing is more common than unsuccessful people with talent. Genius will not; un-rewarded genius is almost a proverb.

No man ever listened himself out of a job.

Never go out to meet trouble. If you just sit still, nine cases out of ten, someone will intercept it before it reaches you.

If I had permitted my failures, or what seemed to me at the time a lack of success, to discourage me, I cannot see any way in which I would have ever made progress.

Work is not a curse; it is the prerogative of intelligence, the only means of manhood, and the measure of civilization.

I want the people of America to be able to work less for the government and more for themselves. I want them to have the rewards of their own industry. That is the chief meaning of freedom.

We made freedom a birthright.

*

Don't expect to build up the weak by pulling down the strong.

*

The fundamental precept of liberty is toleration. We can not permit any inquisition either within or without the law or apply any religious test to the holding of office. The mind of America must be forever free.

*

It is the duty of a citizen not only to observe the law, but to let it be known that he is opposed to its violation.

*

The world has had enough of the curse of hatred and selfishness, of destruction and war. It has had enough of the wrongful use of material power. For the healing of the nations there must be good will and charity, confidence and peace. The time has come for a more practical use of moral power, and more reliance upon the principle that right makes its own might. Our authority among the nations must be represented by justice and mercy. It is necessary not only to have faith, but to make sacrifices for our faith. The spiritual forces of the world make all its final determinations. It is with these voices that America should speak. Whenever they declare a righteous purpose there need be no doubt that they will be heard. America has taken her place in the world as a Republic—free, independent, powerful. The best service that can be rendered to humanity is the assurance that this place will be maintained.

* *

Prosperity is only an instrument to be used, not a deity to be worshipped.

෨

Perhaps one of the most important accomplishments of my administration has been minding my own business.

> # Patriotism is easy to understand in America—it means looking out for yourself by looking out for your country.

One with the law is a majority.

෨

If you don't say anything, you won't be called on to repeat it.

෨

I have never noticed that nothing I never said ever did me any harm.

෨

Four-fifths of all our troubles would disappear, if we would only sit down and keep still.

* *

If you see ten troubles coming down the road, you can be sure that nine will run into the ditch before they reach you.

৲৲

In the discharge of the duties of this office, there is one rule of action more important than all others. It consists in never doing anything that someone else can do for you.

৲৲

The slogan "press on" has solved and always will solve the problems of the human race.

৲৲

Here stands our country, an example of tranquility at home, a patron of tranquility abroad. Here stands its Government, aware of its might but obedient to its conscience. Here it will continue to stand, seeking peace and prosperity, solicitous for the welfare of the wage earner, promoting enterprise, developing waterways and natural resources, attentive to the intuitive counsel of womanhood, encouraging education, desiring the advancement of religion, supporting the cause of justice and honor among the nations. America seeks no earthly empire built on blood and force. No ambition, no temptation, lures her to thought of foreign dominions. The legions which she sends forth are armed, not with the sword, but with the cross. The higher state to which she seeks the allegiance of all mankind is not of human, but of divine origin. She cherishes no purpose save to merit the favor of Almighty God.

Christmas is not a time nor a season, but a state of mind. To cherish peace and goodwill, to be plenteous in mercy, is to have the real spirit of Christmas.

All growth depends upon activity. There is no development physically or intellectually without effort, and effort means work.

We live in an age of science and of abounding accumulation of material things. These did not create our Declaration. Our Declaration created them. The things of the spirit come first. Unless we cling to that, all our material prosperity, overwhelming though it may appear, will turn to a barren scepter in our grasp.

I am the most powerful man in the world, but great power does not mean much except great limitations.

Education is to teach men not what to think but how to think. Government will take on new activities, but it is not more to control the people, the people are more to control the government.

It is conceived that there can be a horizontal elevation of the standards of the nation, immediate and perceptible, by the simple device of new laws. This has never been the case in human experience. Progress is slow and the result of a long and arduous process of self-discipline. Real reform does not begin with a law, it ends with a law.

> In doing good, in walking humbly, in sustaining its own people in ministering to other nations, America will work out its own mighty destiny.

We cannot do everything at once, but we can do something at once.

❧

America is not and must not be a country without ideals. They are useless if they are only visionary; they are only valuable if they are practical. A nation can not dwell constantly on the mountain tops. It has to be replenished and sustained through the ceaseless toil of the less inspiring valleys. But its face ought always to be turned upward; its vision ought always to be fixed on high.

❧

We have been, and propose to be, more and more American. We believe that we can best serve our own country and most successfully discharge our obligations to humanity by continuing to be openly and candidly, intensely and scrupulously, American. If we have any heritage, it has been that. If we have any destiny, we have found it in that direction.

I want the people of all the earth to see in the American flag the symbol of a Government which intends no oppression at home and no aggression abroad, which in the spirit of a common brotherhood provides assistance in time of distress.

≈

In all your deliberations you should remember that the purpose of legislation is to translate principles into action.

≈

No person was ever honored for what he received. Honor has been the reward for what he gave.

≈

Mass demand has been created almost entirely through the development of advertising.

≈

It takes a great man to be a good listener.

≈

There is no dignity quite so impressive, and no independence quite so important, as living within your means.

≈

The President gets the best advice he can find, uses the best judgment at his command, and leaves the event in the hands of Providence.

HERBERT HOOVER

31ST PRESIDENT • 1929–1933

Born: August 10, 1874, in West Branch, Iowa
Died: October 20, 1964, in New York, New York

Wife: Lou Henry

Religion: Society of Friends (Quaker)

Education: Stanford University

Other political offices: Secretary of Commerce

Herbert Hoover worked his way through Stanford, then became a millionaire as a mining engineer before being elected president. At the time of his election, the United States was enjoying a time of unprecedented national prosperity. The stock market crash of 1929 and the Great Depression are linked to his administration. In 1947, fourteen years after he left office, Hoover was appointed by President Truman to be coordinator of the European Food Program and chairman of the Commission for Reorganization of the Executive Branch.

We must not be misled by the claim that the source of all wisdom is in the government.

❧

The durability of free speech and free press rests on the simple concept that it search for the truth and tell the truth.

❧

When there is a lack of honor in government, the morals of the whole people are poisoned.

❧

Every time the government is forced to act, we lose something in self-reliance, character and initiative.

❧

No public man can be just a little crooked. There is no such thing as a no-man's land between honesty and dishonesty.

❧

It is a distressful time for many of our people, but they have shown qualities as high in fortitude, courage, and resourcefulness as ever in our history. With that spirit, I have faith that out of it will come a sounder life, a truer standard of values, a greater recognition of the results of honest effort, and a healthier atmosphere in which to rear our children. Ours must be a country of such stability and security as can not fail to carry forward and enlarge among all the people that abundant life of material and spiritual opportunity which it has represented among all nations since its beginning.

We do not need to burn down the house to kill the rats.

_&_

War is a losing business, a financial loss, a loss of life
and an economic degeneration. . . . It has but few
compensations and of them we must make the most.
Its greatest compensation lies in the possibility that we
may instill into our people unselfishness.

Truth alone can stand the guns of criticism.

It is impossible, my countrymen, to speak of peace
without profound emotion. In thousands of homes in
America, in millions of homes around the world, there
are vacant chairs. It would be a shameful confession of
our unworthiness if it should develop that we have
abandoned the hope for which all these men died.
Surely civilization is old enough, surely mankind is
mature enough so that we ought in our own lifetime to
find a way to permanent peace. Abroad, to west and
east, are nations whose sons mingled their blood with
the blood of our sons on the battlefields. Most of these
nations have contributed to our race, to our culture,
our knowledge, and our progress. From one of them
we derive our very language and from many of them
much of the genius of our institutions. Their desire for
peace is as deep and sincere as our own.

Older men declare war. But it is youth that must fight
and die. And it is youth who must inherit the
tribulation, the sorrow, and the triumphs that are the
aftermath of war.

❧

We have learned that social injustice is the
destruction of justice itself.

❧

Law can not rise above its source in good
citizenship—in what right-minded men most earnestly
believe and desire.

❧

The test of the rightfulness of our decisions must be
whether we have sustained and advanced the ideals of
the American people; self-government in its
foundations of local government; justice whether to
the individual or to the group; ordered liberty;
freedom from domination; open opportunity and
equality of opportunity; the initiative and individuality
of our people; prosperity and the lessening of poverty;
freedom of public opinion; education; advancement of
knowledge; the growth of religious spirit; the tolerance
of all faiths; the foundations of the home and the
advancement of peace.

❧

Those who have a true understanding of America
know that we have no desire for territorial expansion,
for economic or other domination of other peoples.
Such purposes are repugnant to our ideals of human
freedom.

All men are equal before fish.

*

The course of unbalanced budgets is the road to ruin.

*

The greatness of America has grown out of a political and social system and a method of control of economic forces distinctly its own—our American system.

*

Ours is a land rich in resources; stimulating in its glorious beauty; filled with millions of happy homes; blessed with comfort and opportunity. In no nation are the institutions of progress more advanced. In no nation are the fruits of accomplishment more secure. In no nation is the government more worthy of respect. No country is more loved by its people. I have an abiding faith in their capacity, integrity and high purpose. I have no fears for the future of our country. It is bright with hope.

FRANKLIN D. ROOSEVELT

32ND PRESIDENT • 1933–1945
Born: January 30, 1882, in Hyde Park, New York
Died: April 12, 1945, in Warm Springs, Georgia

Wife: Anna Eleanor Roosevelt

Religion: Episcopalian

Education: Harvard College

Other political offices: New York State Senator, Assistant Secretary of the Navy, Governor of New York

Rated by many as our greatest president, Franklin D. Roosevelt greatly expanded the role of government with the New Deal to end the Great Depression. During World War II, Roosevelt, along with Winston Churchill, personally determined Allied military strategy. The only president elected to four terms, Roosevelt died of a brain hemorrhage at the start of his fourth term.

Let me assert my firm belief that the only thing we have to fear is fear itself—nameless, unreasoning, unjustified terror which paralyzes needed efforts to convert retreat into advance.

When you come to the end of your rope, tie a knot and hang on.

There are many ways of going forward, but only one way of standing still.

Confidence . . . thrives on honesty, on honor, on the sacredness of obligations, on faithful protection and on unselfish performance. Without them it cannot live.

The gains in education are never really lost. Books may be burned and cities sacked, but truth, like the yearning for freedom, lives in the hearts of humble men.

True individual freedom cannot exist without economic security and independence. People who are hungry and out of a job are the stuff of which dictatorships are made.

When you see a rattlesnake poised to strike you, do not wait until he has struck before you crush him.

* *

A good leader can't get too far ahead of his followers.

ॐ

It is a terrible thing to look over your shoulder when you are trying to lead—and find no one there.

Happiness . . . lies in the joy of achievement, in the thrill of creative effort.

In the future days which we seek to make secure, we look forward to a world founded upon four essential human freedoms. The first is freedom of speech and expression—everywhere in the world. The second is freedom of every person to worship God in his own way—everywhere in the world. The third freedom is from want . . . —everywhere in the world. The fourth is freedom from fear . . . —anywhere in the world. The world order which we seek is the cooperation of free countries, working together in a friendly, civilized society. This nation has placed its destiny in the hands, heads and hearts of its millions of free men and women, and its faith in freedom under the guidance of God. Freedom means the supremacy of human rights everywhere. Our support goes to those who struggle to gain those rights and keep them. Our strength is our unity of purpose. To that high concept, there can be no end save victory.

A government can be no better than the public opinion which sustains it.

❧

Be sincere, be brief, be seated.

❧

Democracy is not dying. We know it because we have seen it revive—and grow. We know it cannot die—because it is built on the unhampered initiative of individual men and women joined together in a common enterprise—an enterprise undertaken and carried through by the free expression of a free majority.

❧

It is an unfortunate human failing that a full pocketbook often groans more loudly than an empty stomach.

❧

The nation that destroys its soil destroys itself.

❧

And yet we all understand what it is—the spirit—the faith of America. It is the product of centuries. It was born in the multitudes of those who came from many lands—some of high degree, but mostly plain people, who sought here, early and late, to find freedom more freely.

❧

The United States Constitution has proved itself the most marvelously elastic compilation of rules of government ever written.

No man can tame a tiger by stroking it.

America has been the New World in all tongues, to all peoples, not because this continent was a new-found land, but because all those who came here believed they could create upon this continent a new life—a life that should be new in freedom.

I pledge you, I pledge myself, to a new deal for the American people.

We have always known that heedless self-interest was bad morals; we now know that it is bad economics.

The Almighty God has blessed our land in many ways. He has given our people stout hearts and strong arms with which to strike mighty blows for freedom and truth. He has given to our country a faith which has become the hope of all peoples in an anguished world.

Never before have we had so little time in which to do so much.

One thing is sure. We have to do something. We have to do the best we know how at the moment. If it doesn't turn out right, we can modify it as we go along.

We Americans of today, together with our allies, are passing through a period of supreme test. It is a test of our courage—of our resolve—of our wisdom—our essential democracy. If we meet that test—successfully and honorably—we shall perform a service of historic importance which men and women and children will honor throughout all time.

*

The overwhelming majority of Americans are possessed of two great qualities—a sense of humor and a sense of proportion.

*

Because the Nation's needs are greater than ever before, our sacrifices too must be greater than they have ever been before.

*

The hopes of the Republic cannot forever tolerate either undeserved poverty or self-serving wealth. As a matter of fact and law, the governing rights of the States are all of those which have not been surrendered to the national Government by the Constitution or its amendments. Wisely or unwisely, people know that under the eighteenth Amendment Congress has been given the right to legislate on this particular subject, but this is not the case in the matter of a great number of other vital problems of government, such as the conduct of public utilities, of banks, of insurance, of business, of agriculture, of education, of social welfare and of a dozen other important features. In these, Washington must not be encouraged not to interfere.

The presidency is not merely an administrative office. That's the least of it. It is more than an engineering job, efficient or inefficient. It is preeminently a place of moral leadership.

෨

We are fighting to save a great and precious form of government for ourselves and for the world.

෨

Any government, like any family, can for a year spend a little more than it earns. But you and I know that a continuance of that habit means the poorhouse.

෨

I consider it a public duty to answer falsifications with facts. I will not pretend that I find this an unpleasant duty. I am an old campaigner, and I love a good fight.

෨

To stand upon ramparts and die for our principles is heroic, but to sally forth to battle and win for our principles is something more than heroic.

෨

Put two or three men in positions of conflicting authority. This will force them to work at loggerheads, allowing you to be the ultimate arbiter.

෨

The measure of the restoration lies in the extent to which we apply social values more noble than mere monetary profits.

Happiness lies not in the mere possession of money; it lies in the joy of achievement, in the thrill of creative effort. The joy and moral stimulation of work no longer must be forgotten in the mad chase of evanescent profits. These dark days will be worth all they cost us if they teach us that our true destiny is not to be ministered unto but to minister to ourselves and to our fellow men.

≈

The only limit to our realization of tomorrow will be our doubts about reality.

> More than an end to war, we want an end to the beginnings of all wars.

If you treat people right they will treat you right— ninety percent of the time.

≈

We have learned that we cannot live alone, at peace, that our own well-being is dependent on the well-being of other nations, far away. We have learned that we must live as men, and not as ostriches, nor as dogs in the manger. We have learned to be citizens of the world, members of the human community.

We must guard against complacency. We must not underrate the enemy. We must face the fact of a hard war, a long war, a bloody war, a costly war.

જી

This generation of Americans has a rendezvous with destiny.

જી

And every one—every man or woman or child—who bought a War Bond helped—and helped mightily!

જી

Yesterday, December 7, 1941—a date which will live in infamy—the United States of America was suddenly and deliberately attacked by naval and air forces of the Empire of Japan.

જી

If I read the temper of our people correctly, we now realize as we have never realized before our interdependence on each other; that we can not merely take but we must give as well; that if we are to go forward, we must move as a trained and loyal army willing to sacrifice for the good of a common discipline, because without such discipline no progress is made, no leadership becomes effective. We are, I know, ready and willing to submit our lives and property to such discipline, because it makes possible a leadership which aims at a larger good. This I propose to offer, pledging that the larger purposes will bind upon us all as a sacred obligation with a unity of duty hitherto evoked only in time of armed strife.

If I were starting life over again, I am inclined to think that I would go into the advertising business in preference to almost any other. The general raising of the standards of modern civilization among all groups of people during the past half century would have been impossible without the spreading of the knowledge of higher standards by means of advertising.

In politics, nothing happens by accident. If it happens, you can bet it was planned.

It isn't sufficient just to want—you've got to ask yourself what you are going to do to get the things you want.

Let us never forget that government is ourselves and not an alien power over us. The ultimate rulers of our democracy are not a President and senators and congressmen and government officials, but the voters of this country.

Men are not prisoners of fate, but only prisoners of their own mind.

Peace can be made and kept only by the united determination of free and peace-loving peoples who are willing to work together—willing to help one another—willing to respect and tolerate and try to understand one another's opinions and feelings.

* *

Nearly all of us recognize that as intricacies of human relationships increase, so power to govern them also must increase—power to stop evil; power to do good. The essential democracy of our Nation and the safety of our people depend not upon the absence of power, but upon lodging it with those whom the people can change or continue at stated intervals through an honest and free system of elections.

ॐ

Remember you are just an extra in everyone else's play.

ॐ

Selfishness is the only real atheism; aspiration, unselfishness, the only real religion.

ॐ

The liberty of a democracy is not safe if the people tolerate the growth of private power to a point where it becomes stronger than their democratic state itself. That, in its essence, is fascism—ownership of a government by an individual, by a group, or any controlling private power.

ॐ

The virtues are lost in self-interest as rivers are lost in the sea.

ॐ

We can gain no lasting peace if we approach it with suspicion and mistrust or with fear. We can gain it only if we proceed with the understanding, the confidence, and the courage which flow from conviction.

We continue to recognize the greater ability of some to earn more than others. But we do assert that the ambition of the individual to obtain for him a proper security is an ambition to be preferred to the appetite for great wealth and great power.

There is nothing I love as much as a good fight.

> We, too, born to freedom, and believing in freedom, are willing to fight to maintain freedom. We and all others who believe as deeply as we do, would rather die on our feet than live on our knees.

Repetition does not transform a lie into truth.

I ask you to judge me by the enemies I have made.

Hard-headedness will not so easily excuse hardheartedness. We are moving toward an era of good feeling. But we realize that there can be no era of good feeling save among men of good will.

Shall we pause now and turn our back upon the road
that lies ahead? Shall we call this the promised land?
Or, shall we continue on our way? For "each age is a
dream that is dying, or one that is coming to birth."

ॐ

In the field of world policy, I would dedicate this
nation to the policy of the good neighbor.

ॐ

We can afford all that we need; but we cannot afford
all we want.

ॐ

I see a great nation, upon a great continent, blessed
with a great wealth of natural resources. Its hundred
and thirty million people are at peace among
themselves; they are making their country a good
neighbor among the nations. I see a United States
which can demonstrate that, under democratic
methods of government, national wealth can be
translated into a spreading volume of human comforts
hitherto unknown, and the lowest standard of living
can be raised far above the level of mere subsistence.

ॐ

Physical strength can never permanently withstand
the impact of spiritual force.

ॐ

If civilization is to survive, we must cultivate the
science of human relationships—the ability of all
peoples, of all kinds, to live together, in the same world
at peace.

In every land there are always at work forces that drive men apart and forces that draw men together. In our personal ambitions we are individualists. But in our seeking for economic and political progress as a nation, we all go up, or else we all go down, as one people.

In every land there are always at work forces that drive

Lives of nations are determined not by the count of years, but by the lifetime of the human spirit. The life of a man is three-score years and ten: a little more, a little less. The life of a nation is the fullness of the measure of its will to live.

Those who first came here to carry out the longings of their spirit, and the millions who followed, and the stock that sprang from them—all have moved forward constantly and consistently toward an ideal which in itself has gained stature and clarity with each generation.

For more than three centuries we Americans have been building on this continent a free society, a society in which the promise of the human spirit may find fulfillment. Comingled here are the blood and genius of all the peoples of the world who have sought this promise.

In the face of great perils never before encountered, our strong purpose is to protect and to perpetuate the integrity of democracy. For this we muster the spirit of America, and the faith of America.

We shall strive for perfection. We shall not achieve it immediately—but we still shall strive. We may make mistakes—but they must never be mistakes which result from faintness of heart or abandonment of moral principle.

❧

We have plowed the furrow and planted the good seed; the hard beginning is over. If we would reap the full harvest, we must cultivate the soil where this good seed is sprouting and the plant is reaching up to mature growth.

❧

I am not willing that the vitality of our people be further sapped by the giving of cash, of market baskets, of a few hours of weekly work cutting grass, raking leaves, or picking up papers in the public parks. We must preserve not only the bodies of the unemployed from destitution but also their self-respect, their self-reliance, and courage and determination.

❧

Rules are not necessarily sacred, principles are.

❧

Self-interest is the enemy of all true affection.

❧

But the world has grown so small and weapons of attack so swift that no nation can be safe in its will to peace so long as any other powerful nation refuses to settle its grievances at the council table.

Resolute in our determination to respect the rights of others, and to command respect for the rights of ourselves, we must keep ourselves adequately strong in self-defense.

Religion, by teaching man his relationship to God, gives the individual a sense of his own dignity and teaches him to respect himself by respecting his neighbors.

What great crises teach all men whom the example and counsel of the brave inspire is the lesson: Fear not, view all the tasks of life as sacred, have faith in the triumph of the ideal, give daily all that you have to give, be loyal and rejoice whenever you find yourselves part of a great ideal enterprise. You, at this moment, have the honor to belong to a generation whose lips are touched by fire. You live in a land that now enjoys the blessings of peace. But let nothing human be wholly alien to you. The human race now passes through one of its great crises. New ideas, new issues— a new call for men to carry on the work of righteousness, of charity, of courage, of patience, and of loyalty. . . . However memory bring back this moment to your minds, let it be able to say to you: That was a great moment. It was the beginning of a new era. . . . This world in its crisis called for volunteers, for men of faith in life, of patience in service, of charity and of insight. I responded to the call however I could. I volunteered to give myself to my Master—the cause of humane and brave living. I studied, I loved, I labored, unsparingly and hopefully, to be worthy of my generation.

In meeting the troubles of the world we must meet them as one people—with a unity born of the fact that for generations those who have come to our shores, representing many kindreds and tongues, have been welded by common opportunity into a united patriotism.

☙

Investment for prosperity can be made in a democracy.

> Once I prophesied that this generation of Americans had a rendezvous with destiny. That prophecy comes true. To us much is given, more is expected.

This generation will nobly save or meanly lose the last best hope of earth. . . . The way is plain, peaceful, generous, just—a way which if followed the world will forever applaud and God must forever bless.

☙

We must as a united people keep ablaze on this continent the flames of human liberty, of reason, of democracy, and of fair play as living things to be preserved for the better world that is to come.

For national unity is, in a very real and deep sense, the fundamental safeguard of all democracy.

❦

In fulfilling my duty to report upon the state of the Union, I am proud to say to you that the spirit of the American people was never higher than it is today—the Union was never more closely knit together—this country was never more deeply determined to face the solemn tasks before it. The response of the American people has been instantaneous. It will be sustained until our security is assured.

❦

They know that victory for us means victory for the institution of democracy—the ideal of the family, the simple principles of common decency and humanity.

❦

We must, on the other hand, guard against defeatism. That has been one of the chief weapons of Hitler's propaganda machine—used time and again with deadly results. It will not be used successfully on the American people.

❦

Doctrines which set group against group, faith against faith, race against race, class against class, fanning the fires of hatred in men too despondent, too desperate to think for themselves, were used as rabble-rousing slogans on which dictators could ride to power. And once in power they could saddle their tyrannies on whole nations, and on their weaker neighbors.

Our men on the fighting fronts have already proved that Americans today are just as rugged and just as tough as any of the heroes whose exploits we celebrate on the Fourth of July.

❧

We are fighting today for security, for progress and for peace, not only for ourselves, but for all men, not only for one generation but for all generations. We are fighting to cleanse the world of ancient evils, ancient ills.

❧

There never has been—there never can be—successful compromise between good and evil. Only total victory can reward the champions of tolerance and decency and freedom and faith.

❧

The people have now gathered their strength. They are moving forward in their might and power—and no force, no combination of forces, no trickery, deceit, or violence, can stop them now. They see before them the hope of the world—a decent, secure, peaceful life for all men everywhere.

❧

There are as many opinions as there are experts.

❧

I think we consider too much the good luck of the early bird and not enough the bad luck of the early worm. I'm not the smartest fellow in the world, but I can sure pick smart colleagues.

The rest of the world—Ah! there is the rub.

*

Democracy, the practice of self-government, is a covenant among free men to respect the rights and liberties of their fellows.

*

Today the United Nations are the mightiest military coalition in history. They represent an overwhelming majority of the population of the world. Bound together in solemn agreement that they themselves will not commit acts of aggression or conquest against any of their neighbors, the United Nations can and must remain united for the maintenance of peace by preventing any attempt to rearm in Germany, in Japan, in Italy or in any other nation which seeks to violate the Tenth Commandment—Thou shalt not covet.

*

But we have learned that we can never dig a hole so deep that it would be safe against predatory animals. We have also learned that if we do not pull the fangs of the predatory animals of this world, they will multiply and grow in strength and they will be at our throats once more in a short generation.

*

Victory in this war is the first and greatest goal before us. Victory in peace is the next. That means striving toward the enlargement of the security of man here and throughout the world—and, finally, striving for the fourth freedom—Freedom from fear.

As spokesmen for the United States Government, you and I take off our hats to those responsible for our American production—to the owners, managers, and supervisors, to the draftsmen and engineers, to the workers—men and women—in factories and arsenals and ship-yards and mines and mills and forests and railroads and highways. We take off our hats to the farmers who have faced an unprecedented task of feeding not only a great nation but a great part of the world. We take off our hats to all the loyal, anonymous, untiring men and women who have worked in private employment and in Government and who have endured rationing and other stringencies with good humor and good will. We take off our hats to all Americans who have contributed magnificently to our common cause.

First in importance in the American scene has been the inspiring proof of the great qualities of our fighting men. They have demonstrated these qualities in adversity as well as in victory. As long as our flag flies over this Capitol, Americans will honor the soldiers, sailors, and marines who fought our first battles of this war against overwhelming odds—the heroes, living and dead, of Wake and Bataan and Guadalcanal, of the Java Sea and Midway and the North Atlantic convoys. Their unconquerable spirit will live forever.

But I do not think that any of us Americans can be content with mere survival. Sacrifices that we and our allies are making impose upon us all a sacred obligation to see to it that out of this war we and our children will gain something better than mere survival.

The overwhelming majority of our people have met the demands of this war with magnificent courage and understanding. They have accepted inconveniences; they have accepted hardships; they have accepted tragic sacrifices. And they are ready and eager to make whatever further contributions are needed to win the war as quickly as possible—if only they are given the chance to know what is required of them.

*

The point in history at which we stand is full of promise and danger. The world will either move forward toward unity and widely shared prosperity—or it will move apart.

*

There are millions of American men and women who are not in this war at all. It is not because they do not want to be in it. But they want to know where they can best do their share. National service provides that direction. It will be a means by which every man and woman can find that inner satisfaction which comes from making the fullest possible contribution to victory.

*

The test of our progress is not whether we add more to the abundance of those who have much; it is whether we provide enough for those who have little.

*

Human kindness has never weakened the stamina or softened the fiber of a free people. A nation does not have to be cruel to be tough.

I have often said that there are no two fronts for America in this war. There is only one front. There is one line of unity which extends from the hearts of the people at home to the men of our attacking forces in our farthest outposts. When we speak of our total effort, we speak of the factory and the field, and the mine as well as of the battleground—we speak of the soldier and the civilian, the citizen and his Government.

Our men have fought with indescribable and unforgettable gallantry under most difficult conditions, and our German enemies have sustained considerable losses while failing to obtain their objectives.

We Americans of today, together with our allies, are making history—and I hope it will be better history than ever has been made before.

The American people will never stop to reckon the cost of redeeming civilization. They know there never can be any economic justification for failing to save freedom.

The ablest man I ever met is the man you think you are.

❦

Fortunately, American men and women are not easy dupes. Campaigns of group hatred or class struggle have never made much headway among us, and are not making headway now. But new forces are being unleashed, deliberately planned propaganda to divide and weaken us in the face of danger as other nations have been weakened before.

❦

But if the spirit of America were killed, even though the Nation's body and mind, constricted in an alien world, lived on, the America we know would have perished.

❦

It is the task of our generation, yours and mine. But we build and defend not for our generation alone. We defend the foundations laid down by our fathers. We build a life for generations yet unborn. We defend and we build a way of life, not for America alone, but for all mankind. Ours is a high duty, a noble task.

❦

We must be the great arsenal of democracy.

HARRY S. TRUMAN

33RD PRESIDENT • 1945–1953
Born: May 8, 1884 in Lamar, Missouri
Died: December 26, 1972, in Kansas City, Missouri

Wife: Elizabeth "Bess" Virginia Wallace

Religion: Baptist

Education: University of Kansas City Law School

Other political offices: Judge, Jackson County, Missouri; U.S. Senator; Vice President

Harry S. Truman, who worked as a farmer and ran a haberdashery before entering politics, authorized the use of the atomic bomb that brought World War II to an end. During his term of office he was responsible for creating NATO and the Marshall Plan, increasing the minimum wage, and increasing social security benefits.

It is amazing what you can accomplish if you do not care who gets the credit.

❧

When you get an education, that is something nobody can take from you—money is only temporary—but what you have in your head, if you have the right kind of head, stays with you.

❧

A politician is a man who understands government, and it takes a politician to run a government. A statesman is a politician who's been dead ten to fifteen years.

❧

Give me a one-handed economist! All my economists say, "on one hand . . . on the other."

❧

I have found the best way to give advice to your children is to find out what they want and then advise them to do it.

❧

I never give them hell. I just tell the truth, and they think it is hell.

❧

If somebody throws a brick at me, I can catch it and throw it back. But when somebody awards a decoration to me, I am out of words.

Study men, not historians.

✒

You can always amend a big plan, but you can never expand a little one. I don't believe in little plans. I believe in plans big enough to meet a situation which we can't possibly foresee now.

✒

Within the first few months, I discovered that being a president is like riding a tiger. A man has to keep on riding or be swallowed.

✒

I sit here all day trying to persuade people to do the things they ought to have sense enough to do without my persuading them . . . that's all the powers of the president amount to.

✒

I suppose that history will remember my term in office as the years when the Cold War began to overshadow our lives. I have hardly a day in office that has not been dominated by this all-embracing struggle. And always in the background there has been the atomic bomb. But when history says that my term of office saw the beginning of the Cold War, it will also say that in those eight years we have set the course that can win it.

✒

No matter how much the man who sits here may be properly criticized, I hope the critics will once in a while remember that he is the President of the United States as well as a human being.

We must remember that the test of our religious principles lies not just in what we say, not only in our prayers, not even in living blameless personal lives—but in what we do for others.

*

If you can't stand the heat, get out of the kitchen.

*

Secrecy and a free, democratic government don't mix.

We need not fear the expression of ideas—we do need to fear their suppression.

I wonder how far Moses would have gone if he'd taken a poll in Egypt. A pessimist is one who makes difficulties of his opportunities and an optimist is one who makes opportunities of his difficulties.

*

Actions are the seeds of fate. Deeds grow into destiny.

*

America was not built on fear. America was built on courage, on imagination and an unbeatable determination to do the job at hand.

The buck stops here.

❧

Any man who has had the job I've had and didn't have a sense of humor wouldn't still be here.

❧

Carry the battle to them. Don't let them bring it to you. Put them on the defensive and don't ever apologize for anything.

❧

I always remember an epitaph which is in the cemetery at Tombstone, Arizona. It says: "Here lies Jack Williams. He done his damnedest." I think that is the greatest epitaph a man can have—when he gives everything that is in him to do the job he has before him. That is all you can ask of him and that is what I have tried to do.

❧

I have no desire to crow over anybody or to see anybody eating crow, figuratively or otherwise. We should all get together and make a country in which everybody can eat turkey whenever he pleases.

❧

In reading the lives of great men, I found that the first victory they won was over themselves . . . self-discipline with all of them came first. Men make history and not the other way around. In periods where there is no leadership, society stands still. Progress occurs when courageous, skillful leaders seize the opportunity to change things for the better.

The only things worth learning are the things you learn after you know it all.

❧

Upon books the collective education of the race depends; they are the solid instruments of registering, perpetuating and transmitting thought.

❧

When even one American—who has done nothing wrong—is forced by fear to shut his mind and close his mouth—then all Americans are in peril.

❧

The American people stand firm in the faith which has inspired this Nation from the beginning. We believe that all men have a right to equal justice under law and equal opportunity to share in the common good. We believe that all men have the right to freedom of thought and expression. We believe that all men are created equal because they are created in the image of God.

❧

Isolation is the road to a war. Worse than that, isolation is the road to defeat in a war.

❧

I believe that we should make available to peace-loving peoples the benefits of our store of technical knowledge in order to help them realize their aspirations for a better life. And, in cooperation with other nations, we should foster capital investment in areas needing development.

But I say to all men, what we have achieved in liberty, we will surpass in greater liberty.

❧

The plain people of this country found the courage and the strength, the self-discipline, and the mutual respect to fight and to win, with the help of our allies, under God. I doubt if the tasks of the future are more difficult. But if they are, then I say that our strength and our knowledge and our understanding will be equal to those tasks.

❧

Let us all stand together as Americans. Let us stand together with all men everywhere who believe in human liberty.

❧

This is a time for courage, not for grumbling and mumbling.

❧

It's a recession when your neighbor loses his job; it's a depression when you lose your own.

❧

The spirit of the American people can set the course of world history. If we maintain and strengthen our cherished ideals, and if we share our great bounty with war-stricken people over the world, then the faith of our citizens in freedom and democracy will be spread over the whole earth and free men everywhere will share our devotion to those ideals.

Intense feeling too often obscures the truth.

❧

The United States has always had a deep concern for human rights. Religious freedom, free speech, and freedom of thought are cherished realities in our land. Any denial of human rights is a denial of the basic beliefs of democracy and of our regard for the worth of each individual.

❧

This is the hour to rededicate ourselves to the faith in mankind that makes us strong.

❧

The American people have decided that poverty is just as wasteful and just as unnecessary as preventable disease. We have pledged our common resources to help one another in the hazards and struggles of individual life. We believe that no unfair prejudice or artificial distinction should bar any citizen of the United States of America from an education, or from good health, or from a job that he is capable of performing.

❧

The human race has reached a turning point. Man has opened the secrets of nature and mastered new powers. If he uses them wisely, he can reach new heights of civilization. If he uses them foolishly, they may destroy him.

❧

We can control inflation if we make up our minds to do it.

* *

Man must create the moral and legal framework for the world which will insure that his new powers are used for good and not for evil. In shaping the outcome, the people of the United States will play a leading role.

❦

We work for a better life for all, so that all men may put to good use the great gifts with which they have been endowed by their Creator. We seek to establish those material conditions of life in which, without exception, men may live in dignity, perform useful work, serve their communities, and worship God as they see fit.

❦

There is nothing new in the world except the history you do not know.

❦

If you can't convince 'em, confuse 'em.

❦

It should make us truly thankful, as we look back to the beginnings of this country, that we have come so far along the road to a better life for all. It should make us humble to think, as we look ahead, how much farther we have to go to accomplish, at home and abroad, the objectives that were set out for us at the founding of this great Nation. As we approach the halfway mark of the 20th century, we should ask for continued strength and guidance from that Almighty Power who has placed before us such great opportunities for the good of mankind in the years to come.

You can not stop the spread of an idea by passing a law against it.

*

As we meet here today, American soldiers are fighting a bitter campaign in Korea. We pay tribute to their courage, devotion, and gallantry. Our men are fighting, alongside their United Nations allies, because they know, as we do, that the aggression in Korea is part of the attempt of the Russian Communist dictatorship to take over the world, step by step. Our men are fighting a long way from home, but they are fighting for our lives and our liberties. They are fighting to protect our right to meet here today—our right to govern ourselves as a free nation.

*

Let us keep our eyes on the issues and work for the things we all believe in. Let each of us put our country ahead of our party, and ahead of our own personal interests.

*

Peace is precious to us. It is the way of life we strive for with all the strength and wisdom we possess. But more precious than peace are freedom and justice. We will fight, if fight we must, to keep our freedom and to prevent justice from being destroyed.

*

Let us prove, again, that we are not merely sunshine patriots and summer soldiers. Let us go forward, trusting in the God of Peace, to win the goals we seek.

* *

You know that being an American is more than a matter of where your parents came from. It is a belief that all men are created free and equal and that everyone deserves an even break.

The things we believe in most deeply are under relentless attack. We have the great responsibility of saving the basic moral and spiritual values of our civilization. We have started out well—with a program for peace that is unparalleled in history. If we believe in ourselves and the faith we profess, we will stick to that job until it is victoriously finished.

❧

I have a deep and abiding faith in the destiny of free men. With strength and courage, we shall, someday, overcome.

❧

In the great contest in which we are engaged today, we cannot expect to have fair weather all the way. But it is a contest just as important for this country and for all men, as the desperate struggle that George Washington fought through to victory.

The reward of suffering is experience.

This year, 1952, is a critical year in the defense effort of the whole free world. If we falter we can lose all the gains we have made. If we drive ahead, with courage and vigor and determination, we can by the end of 1952 be in a position of much greater security. The way will be dangerous for the years ahead, but if we put forth our best efforts this year—and next year—we can be "over the hump" in our effort to build strong defenses.

Our strength depends upon the health, the morale, the freedom of our people. We can take on the burden of leadership in the fight for world peace because, for nearly 20 years, the Government and the people have been working together for the general welfare. We have given more and more of our citizens a fair chance at decent, useful, productive lives. That is the reason we are as strong as we are today.

The seeds of totalitarian regimes are nurtured by misery and want. They spread and grow in the evil soil of poverty and strife. They reach their full growth when the hope of a people for a better life has died. We must keep that hope alive.

DWIGHT D. EISENHOWER

34TH PRESIDENT • 1953–1961

Born: October 14, 1890, in Denison, Texas
Died: March 28, 1969, in Washington, D.C.

Wife: Mary "Mamie" Geneva Doud

Religion: Presbyterian

Education: West Point

Other political offices: None

A military hero, Dwight D. Eisenhower led the invasion on Normandy in 1943 and was later named as General of the Army. Eisenhower was president of Columbia University before defeating Adlai Stevenson in the race for U.S. president. Eisenhower's term in office was primarily noted for his involvement in foreign policy, but he also sent U.S. troops into Little Rock, Arkansas, during the 1957 segregation crisis. His Interstate Act provided for a 41,000-mile interstate highway system, the single largest public works program in American history.

223

Leadership: the art of getting someone else to do something you want done because he wants to do it.

※

Pull the string, and it will follow wherever you wish. Push it, and it will go nowhere at all.

※

Humility must always be the portion of any man who receives acclaim earned in blood of his followers and sacrifices of his friends.

※

It is the task of statesmanship to mold, to balance, and to integrate these and other forces, new and old, within the principles of our democratic system—ever aiming toward the supreme goals of our free society.

※

No people can live to itself alone. The unity of all who dwell in freedom is their only sure defense.

※

The best morale exists when you never hear the word mentioned. When you hear a lot of talk about it, it's usually lousy.

※

Conceiving the defense of freedom, like freedom itself, to be one and indivisible, we hold all continents and peoples in equal regard and honor. We reject any insinuation that one race or another, one people or another, is in any sense inferior or expendable.

What counts is not necessarily the size of the dog in the fight—it's the size of the fight in the dog.

A people that values its privileges above its principles, soon loses both.

Accomplishments will prove to be a journey, not a destination.

In preparing for battle, I have always found that plans are useless, but planning is indispensable.

In war there is no substitute for victory.

Dollars and guns are no substitutes for brains and will power.

When you are in any contest, you should work as if there were—to the very last minute—a chance to lose it. This is battle. This is politics. This is anything.

Pessimism mever won any battle.

⚜

We feel this moral strength because we know that we are not helpless prisoners of history. We are free men. We shall remain free, never to be proven guilty of the one capital offense against freedom, a lack of staunch faith.

⚜

History does not long entrust the care of freedom to the weak or the timid.

⚜

In the light of this equality, we know that the virtues most cherished by free people—love of truth, pride of work, devotion to country—all are treasures equally precious in the lives of the most humble and of the most exalted.

⚜

Americans, indeed all free men, remember that in the final choice, a soldier's pack is not so heavy a burden as a prisoner's chains.

⚜

This fact defines the meaning of this day. We are summoned by this honored and historic ceremony to witness more than the act of one citizen swearing his oath of service, in the presence of God. We are called as a people to give testimony in the sight of the world to our faith that the future shall belong to the free.

The quest for peace is the statesman's most exacting duty . . . practical progress to lasting peace is his fondest hope.

❧

Every gun that is made, every warship launched, every rocket fired, in a final sense, signifies a theft from those who hunger and are not fed, those who are cold and not clothed.

❧

Mob rule can not be allowed to override the decisions of our courts.

❧

America is best described by one word, freedom.

❧

The older I get, the more wisdom I find in the ancient rule of taking first things first. A process which often reduces the most complex human problem to a manageable proportion.

❧

Only our individual faith in freedom can keep us free.

❧

We cherish our friendship with all nations that are or would be free. We respect, no less, their independence. And when, in time of want or peril, they ask our help, they may honorably receive it; for we no more seek to buy their sovereignty than we would sell our own. Sovereignty is never bartered among freemen.

★ ★

There must be no second-class citizens in this country.

I believe that people in the long run are going to do more to promote peace than our governments. Indeed, I think that people want peace so much that one of these days governments had better get out of their way and let them have it.

જી

I have found out in later years we were very poor, but the glory of America is that we didn't know it then.

જી

There is no victory at bargain basement prices.

જી

We seek victory—not over any nation or people—but over the ancient enemies of us all; victory over ignorance, poverty, disease, and human degradation wherever they may be found.

જી

If we make ourselves worthy of America's ideals, if we do not forget that our nation was founded on the premise that all men are creatures of God's making, the world will come to know that it is free men who carry forward the true promise of human progress and dignity.

Controlled, universal disarmament is the imperative of our time. The demand for it by the hundreds of millions whose chief concern is the long future of themselves and their children will, I hope, become so universal and so insistent that no man anywhere, no government anywhere, can withstand it.

☙

Don't join the book burners. Do not think you are going to conceal thoughts by concealing evidence that they ever existed.

☙

From this day forward, the millions of our schoolchildren will daily proclaim in every city and town, every village and rural schoolhouse, the dedication of our nation and our people to the Almighty.

☙

I could have spoken from Rhode Island where I have been staying, but I felt that in speaking from the house of Lincoln, of Jackson, and of Wilson, my words would better convey the sadness I feel in the action I was compelled today to make and the firmness with which I intend to pursue this course until the orders of the federal court at Little Rock can be executed without unlawful interference.

☙

Organizations cannot make a genius out of an incompetent. On the other hand, disorganizations can scarcely fail to result in efficiency.

I have one yardstick by which I test every major problem—and that yardstick is: Is it good for America?

*

If men can develop weapons that are so terrifying as to make the thought of global war include almost a sentence for suicide, you would think that man's intelligence and his comprehension . . . would include also his ability to find a peaceful solution.

*

It is far more important to be able to hit the target than it is to haggle over who makes a weapon or who pulls a trigger.

*

Neither a wise man nor a brave man lies down on the tracks of history to wait for the train of the future to run over him. The clearest way to show what the rule of law means to us in everyday life is to recall what has happened when there is no rule of law.

*

The supreme quality for leadership is unquestionably Integrity. Without it, no real success is possible, no matter whether it is on a section gang, a football field, in the army, or in an office.

*

There is almost no limit to the human betterment that could result from such cooperation. Hunger and disease could increasingly be driven from the earth. The age-old dream of a good life for all could, at long last, be translated into reality.

The United States pledges its determination to help solve the fearful atomic dilemma—to devote its entire heart and mind to finding the way by which the miraculous inventiveness of man shall not be dedicated to his death but consecrated to his life.

The middle of the road is all of the usable surface. The extremes, right and left, are in the gutters.

Whatever America hopes to bring to pass in the world must first come to pass in the heart of America.

Worry is a word that I don't allow myself to use.

Our real problem, then, is not our strength today, it is rather the vital necessity of action today to ensure our strength tomorrow.

I'm saving the rocker for the day when I feel as old as I really am.

The men who mine coal and fire furnaces and balance ledgers and turn lathes and pick cotton and heal the sick and plant corn—all serve as proudly, and as profitably, for America as the statesmen who draft treaties and the legislators who enact laws.

We must live by what we say.

*

Peace and justice are two sides of the same coin.

Love of liberty means the guarding of every resource that makes freedom possible—from the sanctity of our families and the wealth of our soil to the genius of our scientists.

We are going to have peace, even if we have to fight for it.

*

The peace we seek, then, is nothing less than the practice and fulfillment of our whole faith among ourselves and in our dealings with others. This signifies more than the stilling of guns, easing the sorrow of war. More than escape from death, it is a way of life. More than a haven for the weary, it is a hope for the brave.

*

An intellectual is a man who takes more words than necessary to tell more than he knows.

May the light of freedom, coming to all darkened lands, flame brightly—until at last the darkness is no more. May the turbulence of our age yield to a true time of peace, when men and nations shall share a life that honors the dignity of each, the brotherhood of all.

❧

I hate war only as a soldier who has lived it can, only as one who has seen its brutality, its stupidity.

❧

The world moves, and ideas that were good once are not always good.

❧

We now stand ten years past the midpoint of a century that has witnessed four major wars among great nations. Three of these involved our own country. Despite these holocausts America is today the strongest, the most influential and most productive nation in the world. Understandably proud of this pre-eminence, we yet realize that America's leadership and prestige depend, not merely upon our unmatched material progress, riches and military strength, but on how we use our power in the interests of world peace and human betterment.

❧

The only way to win World War III is to prevent it.

❧

Because we are human we err. But as free men we are also responsible for correcting the errors and imperfections of our ways.

The final battle against intolerance is to be fought—
not in the chambers of any legislature—but in the
hearts of men.

※

Throughout America's adventure in free government,
such basic purposes have been to keep the peace; to
foster progress in human achievement, and to enhance
liberty, dignity and integrity among peoples and
among nations.

※

A vital element in keeping the peace is our military
establishment. Our arms must be mighty, ready for
instant action, so that no potential aggressor may be
tempted to risk his own destruction.

※

Down the long lane of the history yet to be written,
America knows that this world of ours, ever growing
smaller, must avoid becoming a community of dreadful
fear and hate, and be, instead, a proud confederation
of mutual trust and respect.

※

I deplore the need or the use of troops anywhere to
get American citizens to obey the orders of the
constituted courts.

※

The building of such a peace is a bold and solemn
purpose. To proclaim it is easy. To serve it will be hard.
And to attain it, we must be aware of its full meaning—
and ready to pay its full price.

We pray that peoples of all faiths, all races, all nations, may have their great human needs satisfied; that those now denied opportunity shall come to enjoy it to the full; that all who yearn for freedom may experience its spiritual blessings; that those who have freedom will understand, also, its heavy responsibilities; that all who are insensitive to the needs of others will learn charity; that the scourges of poverty, disease and ignorance will be made to disappear from the earth, and that, in the goodness of time, all peoples will come to live together in a peace guaranteed by the binding force of mutual respect and love.

> In every area of political action, free men must think before they can expect to win.

The hope of freedom itself depends, in real measure, upon our strength, our heart, and our wisdom.

For years our citizens between the ages of 18 and 21 have, in time of peril, been summoned to fight for America. They should participate in the political process that produces this fateful summons. I urge Congress to propose to the States a constitutional amendment permitting citizens to vote when they reach the age of 18.

The purpose is clear. It is safety with solvency. The country is entitled to both.

*

And so, I know with all my heart—and I deeply believe that all Americans know—that, despite the anxieties of this divided world, our faith, and the cause in which we all believe, will surely prevail.

*

Our country and its government have made mistakes—human mistakes. They have been of the head—not of the heart. And it is still true that the great concept of the dignity of all men, alike created in the image of the Almighty, has been the compass by which we have tried and are trying to steer our course.

*

Let us proudly remember that the members of the Armed Forces give their basic allegiance solely to the United States. Of that fact all of us are certain.

*

Our greatest hope for success lies in a universal fact: the people of the world, as people, have always wanted peace and want peace now.

*

You do not lead by hitting people over the head—that's assault, not leadership.

JOHN F. KENNEDY

35TH PRESIDENT • 1961–1963

Born: May 29, 1917, in Brookline, Massachusetts
Died: November 22, 1963, in Dallas, Texas

Wife: Jacqueline Lee Bouvier

Religion: Catholic

Education: Harvard College

Other political offices: Member of U.S. House of Representatives, U.S. Senator

A Pulitzer Prize winner for his book, *Profiles in Courage,* John F. Kennedy was the first Roman Catholic to be elected president. Highlights of Kennedy's term in office included his demand that the Soviet Union dismantle its missile bases in Cuba, his civil rights actions, his leadership in space exploration, and his founding of the Peace Corps. He was assassinated on November 22, 1963.

Efforts and courage are not enough without purpose and direction.

꧁

Conformity is the jailer of freedom and the enemy of growth.

꧁

The United States, as the world knows, will never start a war. We do not want a war. We do not now expect a war. This generation of Americans has already had enough—more than enough—of war and hate and oppression. We shall be prepared if others wish it. We shall be alert to try to stop it. But we shall also do our part to build a world of peace where the weak are safe and the strong are just. We are not helpless before that task or hopeless of its success. Confident and unafraid, we labor on—not toward a strategy of annihilation but toward a strategy of peace.

꧁

A man may die, nations may rise and fall, but an idea lives on.

꧁

A man does what he must—in spite of personal consequences, in spite of obstacles and dangers and pressures—and that is the basis of all human morality.

꧁

Our problems are man-made; therefore they may be solved by man. No problem of human destiny is beyond human beings.

Forgive our enemies, but never forget their names.

❧

Yet we can have a new confidence today in the direction in which history is moving. Nothing is more stirring than the recognition of great public purpose. Every great age is marked by innovation and daring— by the ability to meet unprecedented problems with intelligent solutions. In a time of turbulence and change, it is more true than ever that knowledge is power; for only by true understanding and steadfast judgment are we able to master the challenge of history.

❧

Man is still the most extraordinary computer of all.

❧

Leadership and learning are indispensable to each other.

❧

If art is to nourish the roots of our culture, society must set the artist free to follow his vision wherever it takes him.

❧

I want to emphasize in the great concentration which we now place upon scientists and engineers how much we still need the men and women educated in the liberal tradition, willing to take the long look, undisturbed by prejudices and slogans of the moment, who attempt to make an honest judgment on difficult events.

> Happiness: the full use of your powers along the lines of excellence.

Change is the law of life. And those who look only to the past or present are certain to miss the future.

❧

Let us never negotiate out of fear. But let us never fear to negotiate.

❧

When written in Chinese, the word "crisis" is composed of two characters. One represents danger, and the other represents opportunity.

❧

Victory has a thousand fathers but defeat is an orphan.

❧

And so, my fellow Americans: ask not what your country can do for you—ask what you can do for your country.

❧

Too often we . . . enjoy the comfort of opinion without the discomfort of thought.

Let us think of education as the means of developing our greatest abilities, because in each of us there is a private hope and dream which, fulfilled, can be translated into benefit for everyone and greater strength for our nation.

※

The stories of past courage . . . can teach, they can offer hope, they can provide inspiration. But they cannot supply courage itself. For this each man must look into his own soul.

※

There are risks and costs to a program of action, but they are far less than the long-range risks and costs of comfortable inaction.

※

Tolerance implies no lack of commitment to one's own beliefs. Rather it condemns the oppression or persecution of others.

※

If more politicians knew poetry, and more poets knew politics, I am convinced the world would be a little better place in which to live.

※

The quality of American life must keep pace with the quantity of American goods. This country cannot afford to be materially rich and spiritually poor.

It may be different elsewhere. But democratic society—in it, the highest duty of the writer, the composer, the artist is to remain true to himself and to let the chips fall where they may.

The human mind is our fundamental resource.

Those who dare to fail miserably can achieve greatly.

Things do not happen. Things are made to happen.

The time to repair the roof is when the sun is shining.

The problems of the world cannot possibly be solved by skeptics or cynics whose horizons are limited by the obvious realities. We need men who can dream of things that never were.

To exclude from positions of trust and command all those below the age of 44 would have kept Jefferson from writing the Declaration of Independence, Washington from commanding the Continental Army, Madison from fathering the Constitution, Hamilton from serving as secretary of the treasury, Clay from being elected speaker of the House and Christopher Columbus from discovering America.

The greater our knowledge increases, the more our ignorance unfolds.

Let every nation know, whether it wishes us well or ill, we shall pay any price, bear any burden, meet any hardship, support any friend, oppose any foe, to assure the survival and success of liberty.

In the long history of the world, only a few generations have been granted the role of defending freedom in its hour of maximum danger. . . . The energy, the faith, the devotion which we bring to this endeavor will light our country and all who serve it, and the glow from that fire can truly light the world.

In a free society art is not a weapon. . . . Artists are not engineers of the soul.

To state the facts frankly is not to despair the future nor indict the past. The prudent heir takes careful inventory of his legacies and gives a faithful accounting to those whom he owes an obligation of trust.

When power leads man toward arrogance, poetry reminds him of his limitations. When power narrows the area of man's concern, poetry reminds him of the richness and diversity of existence. When power corrupts, poetry cleanses.

The best road to progress is freedom's road.

*

Peace is a daily, a weekly, a monthly process, gradually changing opinions, slowly eroding old barriers, quietly building new structures.

*

It ought to be possible for American consumers of any color to receive equal service in places of public accommodation, such as hotels and restaurants and theaters and retail stores, without being forced to resort to demonstrations in the street, and it ought to be possible for American citizens of any color to register to vote in a free election without interference or fear of reprisal. It ought to be possible, in short, for every American to enjoy the privileges of being American without regard to his race or his color. In short, every American ought to have the right to be treated as he would wish to be treated, as one would wish his children to be treated. But this is not the case.

The cost of freedom is always high, but Americans have always paid it. And one path we shall never choose, and that is the path of surrender, or submission.

* *

We observe today not a victory of a party, but a celebration of freedom—symbolizing an end, as well as a beginning—signifying renewal, as well as change. For I have sworn before you and Almighty God the same solemn oath our forebears prescribed nearly a century and three quarters ago.

⟡

The life of the arts, far from being an interruption, a distraction in the life of a nation, is very close to the center of a nation's purpose—and it is the test of the quality of a nation's civilization.

⟡

Mankind must put an end to war or war will put an end to mankind.

⟡

All free men, wherever they may live, are citizens of Berlin. And therefore, as a free man, I take pride in the words *Ich bin ein Berliner.*

⟡

To those new States whom we welcome to the ranks of the free, we pledge our word that one form of colonial control shall have not passed away merely to be replaced by a far more iron tyranny. We shall not always expect to find them supporting our view. But we shall always hope to find them strongly supporting their own freedom—and to remember that, in the past, those who foolishly sought power by riding the back of the tiger ended up inside.

In the election of 1860, Abraham Lincoln said the question was whether this Nation could exist half slave or half free. In the election of 1960, and with the world around us, the question is whether the world will exist half slave or half free, whether it will move in the direction of freedom, in the direction of the road that we are taking, or whether it will move in the direction of slavery.

If a free society cannot help the many who are poor, it cannot save the few who are rich.

If we meet our responsibilities, I think freedom will conquer. If we fail, if we fail to move ahead, if we fail to develop sufficient military and economic and social strength here in this country, then I think that the tide could begin to run against us, and I don't want historians ten years from now to say, these were the years when the tide ran out for the United States. I want them to say, these were the years when the tide came in, these were the years when the United States started to move again. That's the question before the American people, and only you can decide what you want, what you want this country to be, what you want to do with the future.

I think this is the most extraordinary collection of talent, of human knowledge that has ever been gathered together in the White House, with the possible exception of when Thomas Jefferson dined alone.

Today we are committed to a worldwide struggle to promote and protect the rights of all who wish to be free.

❧

We preach freedom around the world, and we mean it, and we cherish our freedom here at home, but are we to say to the world, and much more importantly, to each other that this is the land of the free except for the Negroes; that we have no second-class citizens except for the Negroes; that we have no class or caste system, no ghettoes, no master race except with respect to Negroes?

❧

I believe this nation should commit itself to achieving the goal, before this decade is out, of landing a man on the moon and returning him safely to earth.

❧

If we cannot end now our differences, at least we can help make the world safe for diversity.

❧

Those who make peaceful revolution impossible will make violent revolution inevitable.

❧

For if we cannot fulfill our own ideals here, we cannot expect others to accept them. And when the youngest child alive today has grown to the cares of manhood, our position in the world will be determined first of all by what provisions we make today—for his education, his health, and his opportunities for a good home and a good job and a good life.

★ ★

> We have the power to make this the best generation of mankind in the history of world, or to make it the last.

Our progress as a nation can be no swifter than our progress in education.

*

The war against hunger is truly mankind's war of liberation.

*

The one unchangeable certainty is that nothing is unchangeable or certain.

*

In its light we must think and act not only for the moment but for our time. I am reminded of the story of the great French Marshal Lyautey, who once asked his gardener to plant a tree. The gardener objected that the tree was slow-growing and would not reach maturity for a hundred years. The Marshal replied, "In that case, there is no time to lose, plant it this afternoon." Today a world of knowledge—a world of cooperation—a just and lasting peace—may be years away. But we have no time to lose. Let us plant our trees this afternoon.

It should be clear by now that a nation can be no stronger abroad than she is at home. Only an America which practices what it preaches about equal rights and social justice will be respected by those whose choice affects our future.

It is an unfortunate fact that we can secure peace only by preparing for war.

Let us not seek the Republican answer or the Democratic answer, but the right answer.

Let both sides seek to invoke the wonders of science instead of its terrors. Together let us explore the stars, conquer the deserts, eradicate disease, tap the ocean depths, and encourage the arts and commerce.

It is an unfortunate fact that we can secure peace only by preparing for war.

For I stand tonight facing west on what was once the last frontier. From the lands that stretch three thousand miles behind me, the pioneers of old gave up their safety, their comfort and sometimes their lives to build a new world here in the West. They were not the captives of their own doubts, the prisoners of their own price tags. Their motto was not "every man for himself"—but "all for the common cause." They were determined to make that new world strong and free, to overcome its hazards and its hardships, to conquer the enemies that threatened from without and within.

Geography has made us [the United States and Canada] neighbors. History has made us friends. Economics has made us partners, and necessity has made us allies. Those whom God has so joined together, let no man put asunder.

History is a relentless master. It has no present, only the past rushing into the future. To try to hold fast is to be swept aside.

Now the trumpet summons us again—not as a call to bear arms, though arms we need; not as a call to battle, though embattled we are—but a call to bear the burden of a long twilight struggle, year in and year out, "rejoicing in hope, patient in tribulation"—a struggle against the common enemies of man: tyranny, poverty, disease, and war itself.

I look forward to an America which will not be afraid of grace and beauty, which will protect the beauty of our natural environment, which will preserve the great old American houses and squares and parks of our national past and which will build handsome and balanced cities for our future.

* *

I hope that no American will waste his franchise and throw away his vote by voting either for me or against me solely on account of my religious affiliation. It is not relevant.

✿

Let us not seek to fix the blame for the past. Let us accept our own responsibility for the future.

✿

I hear it said that West Berlin is militarily untenable— and so was Bastogne, and so, in fact, was Stalingrad. Any danger spot is tenable if men—brave men—will make it so.

✿

America has tossed its cap over the wall of space.

✿

All this will not be finished in the first hundred days. Nor will it be finished in the first thousand days, nor in the life of this administration, nor even perhaps in our lifetime on this planet. But let us begin.

✿

The hopes of all mankind rest upon us—not simply upon those of us in this chamber, but upon the peasant in Laos, the fisherman in Nigeria, the exile from Cuba, the spirit that moves every man and Nation who shares our hopes for freedom and the future. And in the final analysis, they rest most of all upon the pride and perseverance of our fellow citizens of the great Republic.

In a very real sense, it will not be one man going to the
moon, it will be an entire nation. For all of us must
work to put him there.

*

We can help make the world safe for diversity. For in
the final analysis, our most basic common link is that
we all inhabit this small planet. We all breathe the
same air. We all cherish our children's future. And we
are all mortal.

*

My fellow Americans, let us take that first step. Let us
. . . step back from the shadow of war and seek out the
way of peace. And if that journey is a thousand miles,
or even more, let history record that we, in this land at
this time, took the first step.

*

A child miseducated is a child lost.

*

We are not afraid to entrust the American people
with unpleasant facts, foreign ideas, alien philosophies,
and competitive values. For a nation that is afraid to let
its people judge the truth and falsehood in an open
market is a nation that is afraid of its people.

*

I am certain that after the dust of centuries has passed
over our cities, we too, will be remembered not for
victories or defeats in battle or in politics but for our
contributions to the human spirit.

* *

A newly conceived Peace Corps is winning friends and helping people in fourteen countries—supplying trained and dedicated young men and women, to give these new nations a hand in building a society, and a glimpse of the best that is in our country. If there is a problem here, it is that we cannot supply the spontaneous and mounting demand.

જી

The world is very different now. For man holds in his mortal hands the power to abolish all forms of human poverty, and all forms of human life.

જી

The new frontier of which I speak is not a set of promises—it is a set of challenges. It sums up not what I intend to offer the American people, but what I intend to ask of them. It appeals to their pride, not their pocketbook—it holds out the promise of more sacrifice instead of more security.

જી

The great enemy of truth is very often not the lie, deliberate, contrived and dishonest, but the myth, persistent, persuasive and unrealistic.

જી

The goal of education is the advancement of knowledge and the dissemination of truth.

જી

I know there is a God—I see the storm coming and I see his hand in it—if he has a place then I am ready—we see the hand.

The courage of life is often a less dramatic spectacle than the courage of a final moment; but is no less a magnificent mixture of triumph and tragedy.

*

Politics is like football; if you see daylight, go through the hole.

*

And today, having witnessed in recent months a heightened respect for our national purpose and power—having seen the courageous calm of a united people in a perilous hour—and having observed a steady improvement in the opportunities and well-being of our citizens—I can report to you that the state of this old but youthful Union, in the 175th year of its life, is good.

*

We are not lulled by the momentary calm of the sea or the somewhat clearer skies above. We know the turbulence that lies below, and the storms that are beyond the horizon this year. But now the winds of change appear to be blowing more strongly than ever, in the world of communism as well as our own. For 175 years we have sailed with those winds at our back, and with the tides of human freedom in our favor. We steer our ship with hope, as Thomas Jefferson said, "leaving Fear astern." Today we still welcome those winds of change and we have every reason to believe that our tide is running strong. With thanks to Almighty God for seeing us through a perilous passage, we ask His help anew in guiding the "Good Ship Union."

The times are too grave, the challenge too urgent, and the stakes too high—to permit the customary passions of political debate. We are not here to curse the darkness, but to light the candle that can guide us through that darkness to a safe and sane future.

_ß_

But I tell you the New Frontier is here, whether we seek it or not. Beyond that frontier are the uncharted areas of science and space, unsolved problems of peace and war, unconquered pockets of ignorance and prejudice, unanswered questions of poverty and surplus. It would be easier to shrink back from that frontier, to look to the safe mediocrity of the past, to be lulled by good intentions and high rhetoric—and those who prefer that course should not cast their votes for me, regardless of party.

_ß_

My call is to the young in heart, regardless of age—to all who respond to the Scriptural call: "Be strong and of a good courage; be not afraid, neither be thou dismayed."

_ß_

For courage—not complacency—is our need today—leadership—not salesmanship.

_ß_

I look forward to a future in which our country will match its military strength with our moral restraint, its wealth with our wisdom, its power with our purpose.

We dare not forget today that we are the heirs of that first revolution. Let the word go forth from this time and place, to friend and foe alike, that the torch has been passed to a new generation of Americans—born in this century, tempered by war, disciplined by a hard and bitter peace, proud of our ancient heritage—and unwilling to witness or permit the slow undoing of those human rights to which this Nation has always been committed, and to which we are committed today at home and around the world.

*

Those who do nothing are inviting shame as well as violence. Those who act boldly are recognizing right as well as reality.

*

Physical fitness is not only one of the most important keys to a healthy body, it is the basis of dynamic and creative intellectual activity. The relationship between the soundness of the body and the activities of the mind is subtle and complex. Much is not yet understood. But we do know what the Greeks knew: that intelligence and skill can only function at the peak of their capacity when the body is healthy and strong; that hardy spirits and tough minds usually inhabit sound gods.

*

The United States did not rise to greatness by waiting for others to lead. This Nation is the world's foremost manufacturer, farmer, banker, consumer, and exporter.

★ ★

I look forward to an America which will not be afraid of grace and beauty—I look forward to an America that will reward achievement in the arts as we reward achievement in business or statecraft.

But we cannot be satisfied to rest here. This is the side of the hill, not the top. The mere absence of war is not peace. The mere absence of recession is not growth. We have made a beginning—but we have only begun.

❧

This Nation was founded by men of many nations and backgrounds. It was founded on the principle that all men are created equal, and that the rights of every man are diminished when the rights of one man are threatened.

❧

As we press forward on every front to realize a flexible world order, the role of the university becomes ever more important, both as a reservoir of ideas and as a repository of the long view of the shore dimly seen.

As I have said before, not every child has an equal
talent or an equal ability or an equal motivation, but
they should have an equal right to develop their talent
and their ability and their motivation, to make
something of themselves.

☙

Our goal is not the victory of might, but the
vindication of right—not peace at the expense of
freedom, but both peace and freedom, here in this
hemisphere, and, we hope, around the world. God
willing, that goal will be achieved.

☙

My fellow citizens of the world: ask not what America
will do for you, but what together we can do for the
freedom of man.

☙

The heart of the question is whether all Americans
are to be afforded equal rights and equal
opportunities, whether we are going to treat our
fellow Americans as we want to be treated. If an
American, because his skin is dark, cannot eat lunch
in a restaurant open to the public, if he cannot send
his children to the best public school available, if he
cannot vote for the public officials who will represent
him, if, in short, he cannot enjoy the full and free life
which all of us want, then who among us would be
content to have the color of his skin changed and
stand in his place? Who among us would then be
content with the counsels of patience and delay?

★　★

For of those to whom much is given, much is required.
And when at some future date the high court of
history sits in judgment on each one of us—recording
whether in our brief span of service we fulfilled our
responsibilities to the state—our success or failure, in
whatever office we may hold, will be measured by the
answers to four questions. First, were we truly men of
courage—with the courage to stand up to one's
enemies—and the courage to stand up, when
necessary, to one's associates—the courage to resist
public pressure, as well as private greed? Secondly,
were we truly men of judgment—with perceptive
judgment of the future as well as the past—of our own
mistakes as well as the mistakes of others—with
enough wisdom to know that we did not know, and
enough candor to admit it? Third, were we truly men
of integrity—men who never ran out on either the
principles in which they believed or the people who
believed in them—men who believed in us—men
whom neither financial gain nor political ambition
could ever divert from the fulfillment of our sacred
trust? Finally, were we truly men of dedication—with
an honor mortgaged to no single individual or group,
and compromised by no private obligation or aim, but
devoted solely to serving the public good and the
national interest?

LYNDON B. JOHNSON

36TH PRESIDENT • 1963–1969

Born: August 27, 1908, in Johnson City, Texas
Died: January 22, 1973, in Johnson City, Texas

Wife: Claudia "Lady Bird" Alta Taylor

Religion: Disciples of Christ

Education: Southwest Texas State Teachers College

Other political offices: Congressional Secretary, Member of U.S. House of Representatives, U.S. Senator, Vice President

Lyndon B. Johnson became president after Kennedy was assassinated, and won passage of many civil-rights, anti-poverty, aid-to-education, and health-care laws with his Great Society program. To some, however, the escalation of the Vietnam War during Johnson's term and the division it caused throughout the country overshadow his accomplishments.

Yesterday is not ours to recover, but tomorrow is ours to win or lose.

❧

The men who have guided the destiny of the United States have found the strength for their tasks by going to their knees. The private unity of public men and their God is an enduring source of reassurance for the people of America.

❧

The promise of America is a simple promise: Every person shall share in the blessings of this land. And they shall share on the basis of their merits as a person. They shall not be judged by their color, or by their beliefs, or by their religion, or by where they were born, or the neighborhood in which they live.

❧

Once we considered education a public expense; we know now that it is a public investment.

❧

What convinces is conviction. Believe in the argument you're advancing. If you don't you're as good as dead. The other person will sense that something isn't there, and no chain of reasoning, no matter how logical or elegant or brilliant, will win your case for you.

❧

Until justice is blind to color, until education is unaware of race, until opportunity is unconcerned with the color of men's skins, emancipation will be a proclamation but not a fact.

> I believe the destiny of your generation—and your nation—is a rendezvous with excellence.

There are plenty of recommendations on how to get out of trouble cheaply and fast. Most of them come down to this: Deny your responsibility.

❧

We have entered an age in which education is not just a luxury permitting some men an advantage over others. It has become a necessity without which a person is defenseless in this complex, industrialized society. We have truly entered the century of the educated man.

❧

The Negro says, "Now." Others say, "Never." The voice of responsible Americans says, "Together." There is no other way.

❧

Our enemies have always made the same mistake. In my lifetime—in depression and in war—they have awaited our defeat. Each time, from the secret places of the American heart, came forth the faith they could not see or that they could not even imagine. It brought us victory. And it will again.

Any jackass can kick down a barn but it takes a good carpenter to build one.

⟡

They came here—the exiled and the stranger, brave but frightened—to find a place where a man could be his own man. They made a covenant with this land. Conceived in justice, written in liberty, bound in union, it was meant one day to inspire the hopes of all mankind; and it binds us still. If we keep its terms, we shall flourish.

⟡

I am going to build the kind of nation that President Roosevelt hoped for, President Truman worked for, and President Kennedy died for.

⟡

If we fail now, then we will have forgotten in abundance what we learned in hardship: that democracy rests on faith; freedom asks more than it gives, and the judgment of God is harshest on those who are most favored.

⟡

Evil acts of the past are never rectified by evil acts of the present.

⟡

I believe deeply in the ultimate purposes of this Nation—described by the Constitution, tempered by history, embodied in progressive laws, and given life by men and women that have been elected to serve their fellow citizens.

No longer need capitalist and worker, farmer and clerk, city and countryside, struggle to divide our bounty. By working shoulder to shoulder, together we can increase the bounty of all. We have discovered that every child who learns, every man who finds work, every sick body that is made whole—like a candle added to an altar— brightens the hope of all the faithful.

If government is to serve any purpose it is to do for others what they are unable to do for themselves.

This country's ultimate strength lies in the unity of our people.

Under this covenant of justice, liberty, and union we have become a nation—prosperous, great, and mighty. And we have kept our freedom. But we have no promise from God that our greatness will endure. We have been allowed by Him to seek greatness with the sweat of our hands and the strength of our spirit.

The women of America represent a reservoir of talent that is still underused. It is too often underpaid, and almost always underpromoted.

Democracy is a constant tension between truth and half-truth and, in the arsenal of truth, there is no greater weapon than fact.

In establishing preferences, a nation that was built by the immigrants of all lands can ask those who now seek admission: "What can you do for our country?" But we should not be asking: "In what country were you born?" For our ultimate goal is a world without war, a world made safe for diversity, in which all men, goods, and ideas can freely move across every border and every boundary. We must advance toward this goal in 1964 in at least 10 different ways, not as partisans, but as patriots.

❧

I'd rather give my life than be afraid to give it.

❧

We have talked long enough in this country about equal rights. We have talked for one hundred years or more. It is time now to write it in the books of law.

❧

John Kennedy was a victim of hate, but he was also a great builder of faith—faith in our fellow Americans, whatever their creed or their color or their station in life; faith in the future of man, whatever his divisions and differences. This faith was echoed in all parts of the world. On every continent and in every land to which Mrs. Johnson and I traveled, we found faith and hope and love toward this land of America and toward our people.

❧

The great society leads us along three roads—growth and justice and liberation.

As man draws nearer to the stars, why should he not also draw nearer to his neighbors?

✍

For over three centuries the beauty of America has sustained our spirit and has enlarged our vision. We must act now to protect this heritage. In a fruitful new partnership with the States and the cities the next decade should be a conservation milestone. We must make a massive effort to save the countryside and to establish—as a green legacy for tomorrow—more large and small parks, more seashores and open spaces than have been created during any other period in our national history.

✍

A President's hardest task is not to do what is right, but to know what is right.

✍

Peace is a journey of a thousand miles and it must be taken one step at a time.

✍

Even now, a rocket moves toward Mars. It reminds us that the world will not be the same for our children, or even for ourselves in a short span of years. The next man to stand here will look out on a scene different from our own, because ours is a time of change—rapid and fantastic change bearing the secrets of nature, multiplying the nations, placing in uncertain hands new weapons for mastery and destruction, shaking old values, and uprooting old ways.

★ ★

> # Poverty must not be a bar to learning and learning must offer an escape from poverty.

We were never meant to be an oasis of liberty and abundance in a worldwide desert of disappointed dreams. Our Nation was created to help strike away the chains of ignorance and misery and tyranny wherever they keep man less than God means him to be.

A President does not shape a new and personal vision of America. He collects it from the scattered hopes of the American past. It existed when the first settlers saw the coast of a new world, and when the first pioneers moved westward. It has guided us every step of the way. It sustains every President. But it is also your inheritance and it belongs equally to all the people that we all serve. It must be interpreted anew by each generation for its own needs; as I have tried, in part, to do tonight. It shall lead us as we enter the third century of the search for "a more perfect union."

I ask this Congress and this nation to meet our commitments at home and abroad to continue to build a better America and to reaffirm this nation's allegiance to freedom.

Voting is the first dutyof democracy.

❧

Yet as long as others will challenge America's security
and test the dearness of our beliefs with fire and steel,
then we must stand or see the promise of two centuries
tremble. I believe tonight that you do not want me to
try that risk. And from that belief your President
summons his strength for the trials that lie ahead in
the days to come.

❧

The work must be our work now. Scarred by the
weaknesses of man, with whatever guidance God may
offer us, we must nevertheless and alone with our
mortality, strive to ennoble the life of man on earth.

❧

But let us also count not only our burdens but our
blessings—for they are many. And let us give thanks to
the One who governs us all. Let us draw
encouragement from the signs of hope—for they, too,
are many. Let us remember that we have been tested
before and America has never been found wanting. So
with your understanding, I would hope your
confidence, and your support, we are going to
persist—and we are going to succeed.

❧

If ever there was a people who sought more than mere
abundance, it is our people. If ever there was a nation
that was capable of solving its problems, it is this
nation. If ever there were a time to know the pride and
the excitement and the hope of being an American—it
is this time.

★ ★

This administration here and now declares unconditional war on poverty.

✌

I cannot speak to you tonight about Vietnam without paying a very personal tribute to the men who have carried the battle out there for all of us. I have been honored to be their Commander in Chief. The Nation owes them its unstinting support while the battle continues—and its enduring gratitude when their service is done.

✌

I believe, with abiding conviction, that this people—nurtured by their deep faith, tutored by their hard lessons, moved by their high aspirations—have the will to meet the trials that these times impose.

✌

For this is what America is all about. It is the uncrossed desert and the unclimbed ridge. It is the star that is not reached and the harvest sleeping in the unplowed ground. Is our world gone? We say "Farewell." Is a new world coming? We welcome it—and we will bend it to the hopes of man.

RICHARD M. NIXON

37TH PRESIDENT • 1969–1974
Born: January 9, 1913, in Yorba Linda, California
Died: April 22, 1994, in New York, New York

Wife: Thelma "Patricia" Catherine Ryan

Religion: Society of Friends (Quaker)

Education: Whittier College, Duke University Law School

Other political offices: Attorney for U.S. Office of Emergency Management, Member of U.S. House of Representatives, U.S. Senator, Vice President

The first president to visit China, Richard M. Nixon secured a cease-fire in Vietnam and achieved a détente with the Soviet Union. One of the most dramatic events of his first term occurred in 1969, when American astronauts made the first moon landing. Nixon's second term of office was overshadowed by the Watergate scandal, which led to his resignation in 1974.

For years politicians have promised the moon, I'm the first one to be able to deliver it.

A man is not finished when he is defeated. He is finished when he quits.

Only if you have been in the deepest valley can you ever know how magnificent it is to be on the highest mountain.

From this day forward, let each of us make a solemn commitment in his own heart: to bear his responsibility, to do his part, to live his ideals—so that together, we can see the dawn of a new age of progress for America, and together, as we celebrate our 200th anniversary as a nation, we can do so proud in the fulfillment of our promise to ourselves and to the world.

You cannot win a battle in any arena merely by defending yourself.

The greatest honor history can bestow is that of peacemaker.

The peace we seek to win is not victory over any other people, but the peace that comes "with healing in its wings"; with compassion for those who have suffered; with understanding for those who have opposed us; with the opportunity for all the peoples of this earth to choose their own destiny.

*

Baseball is great because anything can happen through the ninth inning.

*

What we need in the spirit of this country and the spirit of our young people is not playing it safe always, not being afraid of defeat—being ready to get into the battle and playing to win, not with the idea of destroying or defeating or hurting anybody else, but with the idea of achieving excellence.

*

And having won some and lost some, I know—as you know—that winning is a lot more fun. But I also know that defeat or adversity can react on a person in different ways. He can give up; he can complain about "a world he never made"; or he can search the lessons of defeat and find the inspiration for another try, or a new career, or a richer understanding of the world and of life itself.

*

Always give your best, never get discouraged, never be petty; always remember, others may hate you. Those who hate you don't win unless you hate them. And then you destroy yourself.

Here is a man [Bart Starr] who did sit on the bench. And instead of whining about it, instead of saying that the coach was at fault or the system was at fault, and quitting or, for that matter, sulking—which seems to be rather a fashionable and common thing to do these days when everything doesn't go your own way—he just kept going along and trying harder, and eventually he came up. And that's what he stands for.

∫ℬ

Unless you try to do your best, unless you give everything that you have to your life and in the service of your country, then you have not been the man or the woman that you can be.

∫ℬ

What really proves that a person or a team or a country has it is not when it is winning and everybody is with it and everybody is cheering it on, but when it has lost one and it does not lose its spirit, it comes back, it comes back and goes on to win.

∫ℬ

It just isn't talent, it isn't physical ability, but that spirit makes a great difference in whether you win or lose.

∫ℬ

The finest steel has to go through the hottest fire.

∫ℬ

We cannot learn from one another until we stop shouting at one another—until we speak quietly enough so that our words can be heard as well as our voices.

A man who has never lost himself in a cause bigger than himself has missed one of life's mountaintop experiences. Only in losing himself does he find himself.

*

All lasting change is incremented, based on unfolding traditions and developing institutions. Revolutionary upheavals may change how the world looks but seldom change the way the world works. Lasting historical change comes not through tidal waves but through the irresistible creeping tide.

*

As this long and difficult war ends, I would like to address a few special words to . . . the American people: Your steadfastness in supporting our insistence on peace with honor has made peace with honor possible.

*

His [Jackie Robinson's] courage, his sense of brotherhood, and his brilliance on the playing field brought a new human dimension not only to the game of baseball but to every area of American life where black and white people work side by side.

*

Once one determines that he or she has a mission in life, that's it's not going to be accomplished without a great deal of pain, and that the rewards in the end may not outweigh the pain—if you recognize historically that always happens, then when it comes, you survive it.

* *

You must never be satisfied with success and you should never be discouraged by failure.

If you take no risks, you will suffer no defeats. But if you take no risks, you win no victories.

My strong point, if I have a strong point, is performance. I always do more than I say. I always produce more than I promise.

೫

Success is not a harbor but a voyage with its own perils to the spirit. The game of life is to come up a winner, to be a success, or to achieve what we set out to do.

೫

Any culture which can put a man on the moon is capable of gathering all the nations of the earth in peace, justice, and concord.

೫

I ask for your support for our brave men fighting tonight halfway around the world, not for territory, not for glory, but that their younger brothers and their sons and your sons can have a chance to grow up in a world of peace and freedom and justice.

Certainly in the next 50 years we shall see a woman president, perhaps sooner than you think. A woman can and should be able to do any political job that a man can do.

✺

For one priceless moment in the whole history of man, all of the people on this earth are truly one. One in their pride at what you [Neil Armstrong] have done, one in our prayers that you will return safely to earth.

✺

If an individual wants to be a leader and isn't controversial, that means he never stood for anything.

✺

If we take the route of the permanent handout, the American character will itself be impoverished.

✺

Sometimes you will apply for a job and you won't get it and you will think it is the greatest setback, but just remember it isn't losing that is wrong; it is quitting. Don't quit. Don't ever quit. Keep trying, because this country needs the very best that you, the young generation of America, can give to it.

✺

Life isn't meant to be easy. It's hard to take being on the top—or on the bottom. I guess I'm something of a fatalist. You have to have a sense of history, I think, to survive some of these things. . . . Life is one crisis after another.

* *

Never let your head hang down. Never give up and sit down and grieve. Find another way. And don't pray when it rains if you don't pray when the sun shines.

※

Never say no when a client asks for something, even if it is the moon. You can always try, and anyhow there is plenty of time afterwards to explain that it was not possible.

※

The man who is aware of himself is henceforward independent; and he is never bored, and life is only too short, and he is steeped through and through with a profound yet temperate happiness.

※

You've got to learn to survive a defeat. That's when you develop character.

The American dream does not come to those who fall asleep.

I know that peace does not come through wishing for it—that there is no substitute for days and even years of patient and prolonged diplomacy.

We have endured a long night of the American spirit. But as our eyes catch the dimness of the first rays of dawn, let us not curse the remaining dark. Let us gather the light.

᠅

Our destiny offers, not the cup of despair, but the chalice of opportunity. So let us seize it, not in fear, but in gladness—and, "riders on the earth together," let us go forward, firm in our faith, steadfast in our purpose, cautious of the dangers; but sustained by our confidence in the will of God and the promise of man.

᠅

The lesson all Americans can learn from Coach [Vince] Lombardi's life is that a man can become a star when, above all else, he becomes an apostle of teamwork.

᠅

Idealism without realism is impotent. Realism without idealism is immoral.

᠅

Let it never be said that because of our failure to present adequately the aims and ideals of freedom, others chose the often irreversible path of dictatorship. Let us speak less of the threat of communism and more of the promise of freedom. Let us adopt as our primary objective not the defeat of communism but the victory of plenty over want, of health over disease, of freedom over tyranny.

GERALD FORD

38TH PRESIDENT • 1974–1977

Born: July 14, 1913, in Omaha, Nebraska

Wife: Elizabeth "Betty" Bloomer Warren

Religion: Episcopalian

Education: University of Michigan, Yale Law School

Other political offices: Member of U.S. House of Representatives, Vice President

After spending twenty-five years in the House of Representatives, Gerald Ford was named vice president after Spiro Agnew resigned. One year later, Ford was named president after the resignation of President Nixon, whom Ford later pardoned. Ford was the first president who had been an Eagle Scout.

My fellow Americans, our long national nightmare is over. Our Constitution works. Our great republic is a government of laws and not of men. Here the people rule.

※

The Constitution is the bedrock of all our freedoms; guard and cherish it; keep honor and order in your own house; and the republic will endure.

※

The American people want a dialogue between them and their president . . . and if we can't have that opportunity of talking with one another, seeing one another, shaking hands with one another, something has gone wrong in our society.

※

I am acutely aware that you have not elected me as your president by your ballots, so I ask you to confirm me with your prayers.

※

A government big enough to give you everything you want is a government big enough to take from you everything you have.

※

It's the quality of the ordinary, the straight, the square, that accounts for the great stability and success of our nation. It's a quality to be proud of. But it's a quality that many people seem to have neglected.

As a people we discovered that our Bicentennial was much more than a celebration of the past; it became a joyous reaffirmation of all that it means to be Americans, a confirmation before all the world of the vitality and durability of our free institutions. I am proud to have been privileged to preside over the affairs of our Federal Government during these eventful years when we proved, as I said in my first words upon assuming office, that "our Constitution works; our great Republic is a Government of laws and not of men. Here the people rule."

Even though this is late in an election year, there is no way we can go forward except together and no way anybody can win except by serving the people's urgent needs. We cannot stand still or slip backwards. We must go forward now together.

America is now stumbling through the darkness of hatred and divisiveness. Our values, our principles and our determination to succeed as a free and democratic people will give us a torch to light the way. And we will survive and become the stronger—not only because of a patriotism that stands for love of country but a patriotism that stands for love of people.

Like President Washington, like the more fortunate of his successors, I look forward to the status of private citizen with gladness and gratitude. To me, being a citizen of the United States of America is the greatest honor and privilege in this world.

Like a runner nearing the end of his course, I hand off
the baton to those who share my belief in America as a
country that has never become, but is always in the act of
becoming. Presidents come and go. But principles
endure, to inspire and animate leaders yet unborn. That is
the message of this Museum [the Gerald Ford Presidential
Library]. That is the mission of every American patriot.
For here the lamp of individual conscience burns bright.
By that light, we can all find our way home.

As I try in my imagination to look into the homes
where families are watching the end of this great
convention, I can't tell which faces are Republicans,
which are Democrats, and which are Independents. I
cannot see their color or their creed. I see only
Americans. I see Americans who love their husbands,
their wives, and their children. I see Americans who
love their country for what it has been and what it must
become. I see Americans who work hard but who are
willing to sacrifice all they have worked for to keep their
children and their country free. I see Americans who in
their own quiet way pray for peace among nations and
peace among themselves. We do love our neighbors,
and we do forgive those who have trespassed against us.
I see a new generation that knows what is right and
knows itself, a generation determined to preserve its
ideals, its environment, our Nation, and the world. My
fellow Americans, I like what I see. I have no fear for
the future of this great country. And as we go forward
together, I promise you once more what I promised
before: to uphold the Constitution, to do what is right
as God gives me to see the right, and to do the very best
that I can for America.

I am proud of America, and I am proud to be an American. Life will be a little better here for my children than for me. I believe this not because I am told to believe it, but because life has been better for me than it was for my father and my mother. I know it will be better for my children because my hands, my brains, my voice, and my vote can help make it happen.

> I believe that truth is the glue that holds government together. Compromise is the oil that makes governments go.

In man's long, upward march from savagery and slavery—throughout the nearly 2,000 years of the Christian calendar, the nearly 6,000 years of Jewish reckoning—there have been many deep, terrifying valleys, but also many bright and towering peaks. One peak stands highest in the ranges of human history. One example shines forth of a people uniting to produce abundance and to share the good life fairly and with freedom. One union holds out the promise of justice and opportunity for every citizen: That union is the United States of America.

As our 200th anniversary approaches, we owe it to ourselves and to posterity to rebuild our political and economic strength. Let us make America once again and for centuries more to come what it has so long been—a stronghold and a beacon-light of liberty for the whole world.

❧

History and experience tell us that moral progress cannot come in comfortable and in complacent times, but out of trial and out of confusion. Tom Paine aroused the troubled Americans of 1776 to stand up to the times that try men's souls because the harder the conflict, the more glorious the triumph.

❧

The truth is we are the world's greatest democracy. We remain the symbol of man's aspiration for liberty and well-being. We are the embodiment of hope for progress. I say it is time we quit downgrading ourselves as a nation. Of course, it is our responsibility to learn the right lesson from past mistakes. It is our duty to see that they never happen again. But our greater duty is to look to the future. The world's troubles will not go away.

❧

My fellow Americans, I once asked you for your prayers, and now I give you mine: May God guide this wonderful country, its people, and those they have chosen to lead them. May our third century be illuminated by liberty and blessed with brotherhood, so that we and all who come after us may be the humble servants of thy peace. Amen. Good night. God bless you.

The oath that I have taken is the same oath that was taken by George Washington and by every President under the Constitution. But I assume the Presidency under extraordinary circumstances never before experienced by Americans. This is an hour of history that troubles our minds and hurts our hearts.

History tells us that it is only a matter of time before your generation is tested—just as ours was tested by economic depression, foreign wars, and the hateful regime of Jim Crow. Outwardly your America may not look the same as mine. New technologies, new forms of communications, new breakthroughs in science and medicine—all these promise to expand the frontiers of life in ways unimaginable just a few short years ago.

JIMMY CARTER

39TH PRESIDENT • 1977–1981
Born: October 1, 1924, in Plains, Georgia

Wife: Eleanor Rosalynn Smith

Religion: Baptist

Education: U.S. Naval Academy

Other political offices: Georgia State Senator, Governor of Georgia

Jimmy Carter was an aide to Admiral Hyman Rickover in the Navy's nuclear submarine program and later returned to Plains, Georgia, to take over the family farm. On his first full day in the Oval Office, Carter pardoned Vietnam draft evaders. He also played a major role in peace negotiations between Israel and Egypt. During his term in office Iranian militants attacked the United States embassy in Teheran. Carter's efforts resulted in the release of the fifty-two hostages taken, shortly after President Reagan took office. Since his retirement, Carter has been active in many human rights causes and Habitat for Humanity.

★ ★

Two centuries ago our nation's birth was a milestone in the long quest for freedom, but the bold and brilliant dream which excited the founders of our nation still awaits its consummation. I have no new dream to set forth today, but rather urge a fresh faith in the old dream.

⟊

Those of us who govern can sometimes inspire, and we can identify needs and marshal resources, but we simply cannot be the managers of everything and everybody.

America did not invent human rights. In a very real sense . . . human rights invented America.

If you fear making anyone mad, then you ultimately probe for the lowest common denominator of human achievement.

⟊

A strong nation, like a strong person, can afford to be gentle, firm, thoughtful, and restrained. It can afford to extend a helping hand to others. It's a weak nation, like a weak person that must behave with bluster and boasting and rashness and other signs of insecurity.

Our American values are not luxuries but necessities—not the salt in our bread but the bread itself. Our common vision of a free and just society is our greatest source of cohesion at home and strength abroad—greater than the bounty of our material blessings.

*

You cannot divorce religious belief and public service. I've never detected any conflict between God's will and my political duty. If you violate one, you violate the other.

*

We must make it clear that a platform of "I hate gay men and women" is not a way to become president of the United States.

*

The law is not the private property of lawyers, nor is justice the exclusive province of judges and juries. In the final analysis, true justice is not a matter of course and law books, but a commitment in each of us to liberty and mutual respect.

*

We must adjust to changing times and still hold to unchanging principles.

*

It has been said that our best years are behind us. But I say again that America's best is still ahead. We have emerged from bitter experiences chastened but proud, confident once again, ready to face challenges once again, and united once again.

As long as I'm President, at home and around the world, America's examples and America's influence will be marshaled to advance the cause of human rights. To establish those values, two centuries ago a bold generation of Americans risked their property, their position, and life itself. We are their heirs, and they are sending us a message across the centuries. The words they made so vivid are now growing faintly indistinct, because they are not heard often enough. They are words like "justice," "equality," "unity," "truth," "sacrifice," "liberty," "faith," and "love." These words remind us that the duty of our generation of Americans is to renew our Nation's faith, not focused just against foreign threats but against the threats of selfishness, cynicism, and apathy.

❧

It is good to realize that if love and peace can prevail on earth, and if we can teach our children to honor nature's gifts, the joys and beauties of the outdoors will be here forever.

❧

The passage of the civil rights acts during the 1960's was the greatest thing to happen to the South in my lifetime. It lifted a burden from the whites as well as the blacks.

❧

One of the most basic principles for making and keeping peace within and between nations . . . is that in political, military, moral, and spiritual confrontations, there should be an honest attempt at the reconciliation of differences before resorting to combat.

Human rights are the soul of our foreign policy,
because human rights are the very soul of our sense of
nationhood.

❧

The passion for freedom is on the rise. Tapping this
new spirit, there can be no nobler nor more ambitious
task for America to undertake on this day of a new
beginning than to help shape a just and peaceful world
that is truly humane.

❧

We are a community, a beloved community, all of us.
Our individual fates are linked, our futures
intertwined. And if we act in that knowledge and in
that spirit, together, as the Bible says, we can move
mountains.

❧

Like music and art, love of nature is a common
language that can transcend political or social
boundaries.

❧

But we know that democracy is always an unfinished
creation. Each generation must renew its foundations.
Each generation must rediscover the meaning of this
hallowed vision in the light of its own modern
challenges. For this generation, ours, life is like nuclear
survival; liberty is like human rights; the pursuit of
happiness is a planet whose resources are devoted to
the physical and spiritual nourishment of its
inhabitants.

* *

Wherever life takes us, there are always moments of wonder.

Our nation can be strong abroad only if it is strong at home. And we know that the best way to enhance freedom in other lands is to demonstrate here that our democratic system is worthy of emulation. I would hope that the nations of the world might say that we had built a lasting peace, built not on weapons of war, but on international policies which reflect our own precious values.

❧

We have no desire to be the world's policeman. But America does want to be the world's peacemaker.

❧

One of those constructive forces is enhancement of individual human freedoms through the strengthening of democracy, and the fight against deprivation, torture, terrorism and the persecution of people throughout the world. The struggle for human rights overrides all differences of color, nation or language. Those who hunger for freedom, who thirst for human dignity, and who suffer for the sake of justice—they are the patriots of this cause. I believe with all my heart that America must always stand for these basic human rights—at home and abroad. That is both our history and our destiny.

The civil rights revolution freed all Americans, black and white, but its full promise still remains unrealized. I will continue to work with all my strength for equal opportunity for all Americans—and for affirmative action for those who carry the extra burden of past denial of equal opportunity.

With these energy and economic policies, we will make America even stronger at home in this decade— just as our foreign and defense policies will make us stronger and safer throughout the world. We will never abandon our struggle for a just and a decent society here at home. That's the heart of America—and it's the source of our ability to inspire other people to defend their own rights abroad.

My decision to register women confirms what is already obvious throughout our society—that women are now providing all types of skills in every profession. The military should be no exception.

The experience of democracy is like the experience of life itself—always changing, infinite in its variety, sometimes turbulent and all the more valuable for having been tested by adversity.

To deal with individual human needs at the everyday level can be noble sometimes.

RONALD REAGAN

40TH PRESIDENT • 1981–1989
Born: February 6, 1911, in Tampico, Illinois

Wives: Jane Wyman; Nancy Davis

Religion: Disciples of Christ

Education: Eureka College

Other political offices: Governor of California

A successful actor before he became governor of California in 1966, Reagan also served as the president of the Screen Actor's Guild for six years. During his terms in Washington, Reagan enacted an economic program that had the largest budget and tax cuts in history. Overseas, Reagan sent a task force to lead the invasion of Grenada, maintained peacekeeping forces in Lebanon, and held four summits with Soviet leader Mikhail Gorbachev, which led to a historic treaty that eliminated short- and medium-range missiles in Europe.

Trust the people—that is the crucial lesson of history.

America is too great for small dreams.

My philosophy of life is that if we make up our mind what we are going to make of our lives, then work hard toward that goal, we never lose—somehow we win out.

Surround yourself with the best people you can find, delegate authority, and don't interfere.

While I take inspiration from the past, like most Americans, I live for the future.

A leader, once convinced a particular course of action is the right one, must have the determination to stick with it and be undaunted when the going gets rough.

I want to say something to the schoolchildren of America who were watching the live coverage of the shuttle's takeoff. I know it is hard to understand, but sometimes painful things like this happen. It's all part of the process of exploration and discovery. It's all part of taking a chance and expanding man's horizons. The future doesn't belong to the fainthearted; it belongs to the brave. The Challenger crew was pulling us into the future, and we'll continue to follow them.

> Excellence demands competition. Without a race there can be no champion, no records broken, no excellence—in education or in any other walk of life.

There are no such things as limits to growth, because there are no limits on the human capacity for intelligence, imagination and wonder.

ॐ

Peace is more than just the absence of war. True peace is justice. True peace is freedom. And true peace dictates the recognition of human rights.

ॐ

No arsenal or no weapon in the arsenals of the world is so formidable as the will and moral courage of free men and women.

ॐ

What brought America back? The American people brought us back—with quiet courage and common sense; with undying faith that in this Nation under God the future will be ours, for the future belongs to the free.

There can be no real peace while one American is dying some place in the world [Vietnam] for the rest of us. We are at war with the most dangerous enemy that has ever faced mankind in his long climb from the swamp to the stars, and it has been said if we lost that war, and in doing so lost this way of freedom of ours, history will record with the greatest astonishment that those who had the most to lose did the least to prevent its happening. . . . If we lose freedom here, there is no place to escape to. This is the last stand on Earth.

❧

The march of freedom and democracy . . . will leave Marxism-Leninism on the ash heap of history as it has left other tyrannies which stifle the freedom and muzzle the self-expression of the people.

❧

I believe that communism is another sad, bizarre chapter in human history whose last pages even now are being written. I believe this because the source of our strength in the quest for human freedom is not material, but spiritual. And because it knows no limitation, it must terrify and ultimately triumph over those who would enslave their fellow man.

❧

Democracy is worth dying for, because it's the most deeply honorable form of government ever devised by man.

❧

In America, our origins matter less than our destination, and that is what democracy is all about.

The American dream is not that every man must be level with every other man. The American dream is that every man must be free to become whatever God intends he should become.

❧

The house we hope to build is not for my generation but for yours. It is your future that matters. And I hope that when you are my age, you will be able to say as I have been able to say: We lived in freedom. We lived lives that were a statement, not an apology.

❧

We will always remember. We will always be proud. We will always be prepared, so we may always be free.

❧

As we renew ourselves here in our own land, we will be seen as having greater strength throughout the world. We will again be the example of freedom and a beacon of hope for those who do not now have freedom.

❧

You and I are told we must choose between a left or right, but I suggest there is no such thing as a left or right. There is only an up or down. Up to man's age-old dream—the maximum of individual freedom consistent with order—or down to the ant heap of totalitarianism. Regardless of their sincerity, their humanitarian motives, those who would sacrifice freedom for security have embarked on this downward path. Plutarch warned, "The real destroyer of the liberties of the people is he who spreads among them bounties, donations and benefits."

Concentrated power has always been the enemy of liberty.

❧

We believed then and now there are no limits to growth and human progress when men and women are free to follow their dreams.

❧

America must remain freedom's staunchest friend, for freedom is our best ally.

❧

Freedom is one of the deepest and noblest aspirations of the human spirit. People, worldwide, hunger for the right of self-determination, for those inalienable rights that make for human dignity and progress.

❧

It is not my intention to do away with government. It is rather to make it work—work with us, not over us; stand by our side, not ride on our back. Government can and must provide opportunity, not smother it; foster productivity, not stifle it.

❧

And let me offer lesson number one about America: All great change in America begins at the dinner table. So, tomorrow night in the kitchen I hope the talking begins. And children, if your parents haven't been teaching you what it means to be an American, let 'em know and nail 'em on it. That would be a very American thing to do.

We who live in free market societies believe that growth, prosperity and ultimately human fulfillment, are created from the bottom up, not the government down. Only when the human spirit is allowed to invent and create, only when individuals are given a personal stake in deciding economic policies and benefiting from their success—only then can societies remain economically alive, dynamic, progressive, and free. Trust the people. This is the one irrefutable lesson of the entire postwar period, contradicting the notion that rigid government controls are essential to economic development.

Government has an important role in helping develop a country's economic foundation. But the critical test is whether government is genuinely working to liberate individuals by creating incentives to work, save, invest, and succeed.

I call upon the scientific community in our country, those who gave us nuclear weapons, to turn their great talents now to the cause of mankind and world peace, to give us the means of rendering those nuclear weapons impotent and obsolete.

The men of Normandy had faith that what they were doing was right, faith that they fought for all humanity, faith that a just God would grant them mercy on this beachhead or the next. It was the deep knowledge— and pray God we have not lost it—that there is a profound moral difference between the use of force for liberation and the use of force for conquest.

★ ★

We will never forget them [the men and women on the space shuttle *Challenger*], nor the last time we saw them—this morning, as they prepared for their journey, and waved good-bye, and "slipped the surly bonds of earth" to "touch the face of God."

≈

It's time we asked ourselves if we still know the freedoms intended for us by the Founding Fathers. James Madison said, "We base all our experiments on the capacity of mankind for self-government." This idea that government was beholden to the people, that it had no other source of power, is still the newest, most unique idea in all the long history of man's relation to man. This is the issue of this election: Whether we believe in our capacity for self-government or whether we abandon the American Revolution and confess that a little intellectual elite in a far-distant capital can plan our lives for us better than we can plan them ourselves.

≈

Now, as most of you know, I'm not one for looking back. I figure there will be plenty of time for that when I get old. But rather, what I take from the past is inspiration for the future, and what we accomplished during our years at the White House must never be lost amid the rhetoric of political revisionists.

≈

Don't let anyone tell you that America's best days are behind her—that the American spirit has been vanquished. We've seen it triumph too often in our lives to stop believing in it now.

The poet called Miss Liberty's torch, "the lamp beside the golden door." Well, that was the entrance to America, and it still is. . . . The glistening hope of that lamp is still ours. Every promise, every opportunity is still golden in this land. And through that golden door our children can walk into tomorrow with the knowledge that no one can be denied the promise that is America. Her heart is full; her torch is still golden, her future bright. She has arms big enough to comfort and strong enough to support, for the strength in her arms is the strength of her people. She will carry on in the eighties unafraid, unashamed, and unsurpassed. In this springtime of hope, some lights seem eternal; America's is.

> I know it's hard when you're up to your armpits in alligators to remember you came here to drain the swamp.

The challenge of statesmanship is to have the vision to dream of a better, safer world and the courage, persistence, and patience to turn that dream into reality.

✺

I've always believed that a lot of the trouble in the world would disappear if we were talking to each other instead of about each other.

We in government should learn to look at our country with the eyes of the entrepreneur, seeing possibilities where others see only problems.

*

It is up to us . . . to work together for progress and humanity so that our grandchildren, when they look back at us, can truly say that we not only preserved the flame of freedom, but cast its warmth and light further than those who came before us.

*

Peace is the highest aspiration of the American people. We will negotiate for it, sacrifice for it; we will never surrender for it, now or ever.

*

There is no question that we have failed to live up to the dreams of the founding fathers many times and in many places. Sometimes we do better than others. But all in all, the one thing we must be on guard against is thinking that because of this, the system has failed. The system has not failed. Some human beings have failed the system.

*

Let us resolve that we the people will build an American opportunity society in which all of us—white and black, rich and poor, young and old—will go forward together arm in arm. Again, let us remember that though our heritage is one of bloodlines from every corner of the Earth, we are all Americans pledged to carry on this last, best hope of man on Earth.

They say the world has become too complex for simple answers. They are wrong. There are no easy answers, but there are simple answers. We must have the courage to do what we know is morally right.

❧

The work of volunteer groups throughout our country represents the very heart and soul of America. They have helped make this the most compassionate, generous, and humane society that ever existed on the face of this earth.

❧

We are the showcase of the future. And it is within our power to mold that future—this year and for decades to come. It can be as grand and as great as we make it. No crisis is beyond the capacity of our people to solve; no challenge too great.

❧

This country was founded and built by people with great dreams and the courage to take great risks.

❧

With our eyes fixed on the future, but recognizing the realities of today . . . we will achieve our destiny to be as a shining city on a hill for all mankind to see.

❧

The ultimate determinant in the struggle now going on for the world will not be bombs and rockets but a test of wills and ideas—a trial of spiritual resolve; the values we hold, the beliefs we cherish and the ideas to which we are dedicated.

My belief has always been . . . that wherever in this land any individual's constitutional rights are being unjustly denied, it is the obligation of the federal government—at point of bayonet if necessary—to restore that individual's constitutional rights.

₰

I hope we have once again reminded people that man is not free unless government is limited. There's a clear cause and effect here that is as neat and predictable as a law of physics: as government expands, liberty contracts.

₰

Facts are stubborn things.

₰

I favor the Civil Rights Act of 1964 and it must be enforced at gunpoint if necessary.

₰

The glory of this land has been its capacity for transcending the moral evils of our past. For example, the long struggle of minority citizens for equal rights, once a source of disunity and civil war, is now a point of pride for all Americans. We must never go back. There is no room for racism, anti-Semitism, or other forms of ethnic and racial hatred in this country.

₰

And you young people out there, don't ever forget that. Some day, you could be in this room—but wherever you are, America is depending on you to reach your highest and be your best because here, in America, we the people are in charge.

History is a ribbon, always unfurling; history is a journey. And as we continue our journey, we think of those who traveled before us. We stand together again at the steps of this symbol of our democracy—or we would have been standing at the steps if it hadn't gotten so cold. Now we are standing inside this symbol of our democracy. Now we hear again the echoes of our past: a general falls to his knees in the hard snow of Valley Forge; a lonely President paces the darkened halls, and ponders his struggle to preserve the Union; the men of the Alamo call out encouragement to each other; a settler pushes west and sings a song, and the song echoes out forever and fills the unknowing air. It is the American sound. It is hopeful, big-hearted, idealistic, daring, decent, and fair. That's our heritage; that is our song. We sing it still. For all our problems, our differences, we are together as of old, as we raise our voices to the God who is the Author of this most tender music. And may He continue to hold us close as we fill the world with our sound—sound in unity, affection, and love—one people under God, dedicated to the dream of freedom that He has placed in the human heart, called upon now to pass that dream on to a waiting and hopeful world.

Let it be said of us that we, too, did not fail. That we, too, worked together to bring America through difficult times. Let us so conduct ourselves that two centuries from now, another Congress and another President, meeting in this Chamber as we are meeting, will speak of us with pride, saying that we met the test and preserved for them in their day the sacred flame of liberty—this last, best hope of man on Earth.

> Let us be sure that those who come after will say of us in our time, that in our time we did everything that could be done. We finished the race; we kept them free; we kept the faith.

The American Dream is a song of hope that rings through night winter air. Vivid, tender music that warms our hearts when the least among us aspire to the greatest things—to venture daring enterprises; to unearth new beauty in music, literature, and art; to discover a new universe inside a tiny silicon chip or a single human cell.

*

Government is the people's business and every man, woman and child becomes a shareholder with the first penny of tax paid.

*

We are creating a nation once again vibrant, robust, and alive. But there are many mountains yet to climb. We will not rest until every American enjoys the fullness of freedom, dignity, and opportunity as our birthright. It is our birthright as citizens of this great Republic, and we'll meet this challenge.

* *

We have a long way to go, but thanks to the courage, patience, and strength of our people, America is on the mend.

୬ℬ⌐

We did not seek the role of leadership that has been thrust upon us. But whether we like it or not, the events of our time demand America's participation.

୬ℬ⌐

We have every right to dream heroic dreams. Those who say that we are in a time when there are no heroes just don't know where to look. You can see heroes every day going in and out of factory gates. Others, a handful in number, produce enough food to feed all of us and then the world beyond. You meet heroes across a counter—and they are on both sides of that counter. There are entrepreneurs with faith in themselves and faith in an idea who create new jobs, new wealth and opportunity. They are individuals and families whose taxes support the Government and whose voluntary gifts support church, charity, culture, art, and education. Their patriotism is quiet but deep. Their values sustain our national life.

୬ℬ⌐

You and I have a rendezvous with destiny. We will preserve for our children this, the last best hope of man on earth, or we will sentence them to take the first step into a thousand years of darkness. If we fail, at least let our children and our children's children say of us we justified our brief moment here. We did all that could be done.

GEORGE BUSH

41ST PRESIDENT • 1989–1993

Born: June 12, 1924, in Milton, Massachusetts

Wife: Barbara Pierce

Religion: Episcopalian

Education: Yale University

Other political offices: Member of U.S. House of Representatives, Ambassador to the United Nations, Director of the CIA, Vice President

George Bush is the son of U.S. Senator Prescott Bush and the father of George W. Bush, the forty-third president. Bush sent forces to the Persian Gulf in response to Iraq's invasion of Kuwait. He also sent to Panama the armed forces that captured military strongman Manuel Noriega. A former director of the CIA, Bush supported Soviet reforms and Eastern European democratization.

Leadership to me means duty, honor, country. It means character, and it means listening from time to time.

≈

Use power to help people. For we are given power not to advance our own purposes, nor to make a great show in the world, nor a name. There is but one just use of power and it is to serve people.

≈

We know what works: freedom works. We know what's right: freedom is right. We know how to secure a more and just and prosperous life for man on earth: through free markets, free speech, free elections and the exercise of free will unhampered by the state.

≈

America today is a proud, free nation, decent and civil, a place we cannot help but love.

≈

I want a kinder, gentler nation.

≈

This is a fact: strength in the pursuit of peace is no vice; isolation in the pursuit of security is no vice.

≈

Let future generations understand the burden and the blessings of freedom. Let them say we stood where duty required us to stand. Let them know that, together, we affirmed America and the world as a community of conscience.

For more than forty years, America and its allies held communism in check and insured that democracy would continue to exist. And today, with communism crumbling, our aim must be to insure democracy's advance, to take the lead in forging peace and freedom's best hope, a great and growing commonwealth of free nations.

This is America . . . a brilliant diversity spread like stars. Like a thousand points of light in a broad and peaceful sky.

Some see leadership as high drama, and the sound of trumpets calling, and sometimes it is that. But I see history as a book with many pages, and each day we fill a page with acts of hopefulness and meaning. The new breeze blows, a page turns, the story unfolds. And so today a chapter begins, a small and stately story of unity, diversity, and generosity—shared, and written, together.

If anyone tells you that America's best days are behind her, they're looking the wrong way.

A government that remembers that the people are its master is a good and needed thing.

I take as my guide the hope of a saint: in crucial things, unity; in important things, diversity; in all things, generosity.

You do not reform a world by ignoring it.

But let me tell you, this gender thing is history. You're looking at a guy who sat down with Margaret Thatcher across the table and talked about serious issues.

From now on, any definition of a successful life must include serving others.

We don't want an America that is closed to the world. What we want is a world that is open to America.

The long roll call, all the G.I. Joes and Janes, all the ones who fought faithfully for freedom, who hit the ground and sucked the dust and knew their share of horror. This may seem frivolous, and I don't mean it so, but it's moving to me how the world saw them. The world saw not only their special valor but their special style: their rambunctious, optimistic bravery, their do-or-die unity unhampered by class or race or region. What a group we've put forth, for generations now, from the ones who wrote "Kilroy was here" on the walls of the German stalags to those who left signs in the Iraqi desert that said, "I saw Elvis." What a group of kids we've sent out into the world.

I come before you and assume the Presidency at a
moment rich with promise. We live in a peaceful,
prosperous time, but we can make it better. For a new
breeze is blowing, and a world refreshed by freedom
seems reborn; for in man's heart, if not in fact, the day
of the dictator is over. The totalitarian era is passing, its
old ideas blown away like leaves from an ancient, lifeless
tree. A new breeze is blowing, and a nation refreshed by
freedom stands ready to push on. There is new ground
to be broken, and new action to be taken. There are
times when the future seems thick as a fog; you sit and
wait, hoping the mists will lift and reveal the right path.
But this is a time when the future seems a door you can
walk right through into a room called tomorrow.

Great nations like great men must keep their word.
When America says something, America means it,
whether a treaty or an agreement or a vow made on
marble steps. We will always try to speak clearly, for
candor is a compliment, but subtlety, too, is good and
has its place.

Moods come and go, but greatness endures. Ours
does. And maybe for a moment it's good to remember
what, in the dailyness of our lives, we forget: We are
still and ever the freest nation on Earth, the kindest
nation on Earth, the strongest nation on Earth. And
we have always risen to the occasion. And we are going
to lift this Nation out of hard times inch by inch and
day by day, and those who would stop us had better
step aside. Because I look at hard times, and I make
this vow: This will not stand.

There is much to do; and tomorrow the work begins. I do not mistrust the future; I do not fear what is ahead. For our problems are large, but our heart is larger. Our challenges are great, but our will is greater. And if our flaws are endless, God's love is truly boundless.

And so, tonight I'm going to ask something of every one of you. Now, let me start with my generation, with the grandparents out there. You are our living link to the past. Tell your grandchildren the story of struggles waged at home and abroad, of sacrifices freely made for freedom's sake. And tell them your own story as well, because every American has a story to tell. And, parents, your children look to you for direction and guidance. Tell them of faith and family. Tell them we are one nation under God. Teach them that of all the many gifts they can receive liberty is their most precious legacy, and of all the gifts they can give the greatest is helping others. And to the children and young people out there tonight: With you rests our hope, all that America will mean in the years and decades ahead. Fix your vision on a new century—your century, on dreams we cannot see, on the destiny that is yours and yours alone.

We are not the sum of our possessions.

America is never wholly herself unless she is engaged in high moral principle. We as a people have such a purpose today. It is to make kinder the face of the nation and gentler the face of the world.

We in this Union enter the last decade of the 20th
century thankful for our blessings, steadfast in our
purpose, aware of our difficulties, and responsive to
our duties at home and around the world. For two
centuries, America has served the world as an inspiring
example of freedom and democracy. For generations,
America has led the struggle to preserve and extend
the blessings of liberty. And today, in a rapidly
changing world, American leadership is indispensable.
Americans know that leadership brings burdens and
sacrifices. But we also know why the hopes of humanity
turn to us. We are Americans; we have a unique
responsibility to do the hard work of freedom. And
when we do, freedom works.

*

Democracy belongs to us all, and freedom is like a
beautiful kite than can go higher and higher with the
breeze.

*

Yes, the United States bears a major share of
leadership in this effort. Among the nations of the
world, only the United States of America has both the
moral standing and the means to back it up. We're the
only nation on this Earth that could assemble the
forces of peace. This is the burden of leadership and
the strength that has made America the beacon of
freedom in a searching world.

BILL CLINTON

42ND PRESIDENT • 1993–2001
Born: August 19, 1946, in Hope, Arkansas

Wife: Hillary Rodham

Religion: Baptist

Education: Georgetown University, Yale Law School

Other political offices: Arkansas Attorney General, Governor of Arkansas

A five-term governor of Arkansas, Bill Clinton oversaw one of the greatest periods of economic prosperity in American history. During his terms, Clinton balanced the budget, significantly reformed welfare, and led peacekeeping efforts around the globe.

★ ★

At the dawn of the 21st century, a free people must now choose to shape the forces of the Information Age and the global society, to unleash the limitless potential of all our people, and yes, to form a more perfect union.

❧

America demands and deserves big things from us— and nothing big ever came from being small.

❧

I want to build a bridge to the 21st century in which we expand opportunity through education, where computers are as much a part of the classroom as blackboards, where highly trained teachers demand peak performance from our students, where every eight-year-old can point to a book and say, "I can read it myself."

❧

Of course, you can't gain ground if you are standing still.

❧

I like the job. That's what I'll miss the most . . . I'm not sure anybody ever liked this as much as I've liked it.

❧

Tonight I ask everyone in this Chamber—and every American—to look into their hearts, spark their hopes, and fire their imaginations. There is so much good, so much possibility, so much excitement in our nation. If we act boldly, as leaders should, our legacy will be one of progress and prosperity. This, then, is America's new direction. Let us summon the courage to seize the day.

★ ★

Each generation of Americans must define what it means to be an American.

୬୭

The real differences around the world today are not between Jews and Arabs; Protestants and Catholics; Muslims, Croats, and Serbs. The real differences are between those who embrace peace and those who destroy it; between those who look to the future and those who cling to the past; between those who open their arms and those who are determined to clench their fists.

୬୭

You know, when the framers finished crafting our Constitution in Philadelphia, Benjamin Franklin stood in Independence Hall and he reflected on the carving of the sun that was on the back of a chair he saw. The sun was low on the horizon. So he said this—he said, "I've often wondered whether that sun was rising or setting. Today," Franklin said, " I have the happiness to know it's a rising sun." Today, because each succeeding generation of Americans has kept the fire of freedom burning brightly, lighting those frontiers of possibility, we all still bask in the glow and the warmth of Mr. Franklin's sun.

୬୭

May those generations whose faces we cannot yet see, whose names we may never know, say of us here that we led our beloved land into a new century with the American Dream alive for all her children; with the American promise of a more perfect union a reality for all her people; with America's bright flame of freedom spreading throughout the world.

Never pick a fight with people who buy ink by the barrel.

❧

The promise of America was born in the 18th century out of the bold conviction that we are all created equal. It was extended and preserved in the 19th century, when our nation spread across the continent, saved the union, and abolished the awful scourge of slavery.

❧

Today, a generation raised in the shadows of the Cold War assumes new responsibilities in a world warmed by the sunshine of freedom but threatened still by ancient hatreds and new plagues.

❧

But our greatest strength is the power of our ideas, which are still new in many lands. Across the world, we see them embraced—and we rejoice. Our hopes, our hearts, our hands, are with those on every continent who are building democracy and freedom. Their cause is America's cause.

❧

And so I say to you tonight, let's give our children a future. Let us take away their guns and give them books. Let us overcome their despair and replace it with hope. Let us, by our example, teach them to obey the law, respect our neighbors, and cherish our values. Let us weave these sturdy threads into a new American community that can once more stand strong against the forces of despair and evil because everybody has a chance to walk into a better tomorrow.

★ ★

It takes a long time to turn a big country around. Just be of good cheer and keep working on it.

✐

The new rage is to say that the government is the cause of all our problems, and if only we had no government, we'd have no problems. I can tell you, that contradicts evidence, history, and common sense.

There is nothing wrong with America that cannot be cured with what is right in America.

To realize the full possibilities of this economy, we must reach beyond our own borders, to shape the revolution that is tearing down barriers and building new networks among nations and individuals, and economies and cultures: globalization. It's the central reality of our time.

✐

When I took office, only high energy physicists had ever heard of what is called the Worldwide Web. . . . Now even my cat has its own page.

✐

Our objectives are clear. Our forces are strong, and our cause is right.

Now, each of us must hold high the torch of citizenship in our own lives. None of us can finish the race alone. We can only achieve our destiny together— one hand, one generation, one American connecting to another. There have always been things we could do together—dreams we could make real—which we could never have done on our own. We Americans have forged our identity, our very union, from every point of view and every point on the planet, every different opinion. But we must be bound together by a faith more powerful than any doctrine that divides us—by our belief in progress, our love of liberty, and our relentless search for common ground.

℘

They [veterans of the Allied landing in Normandy] may walk with a little less spring in their step, and the ranks are growing thinner, but let us never forget, when they were young, these men saved the world.

℘

For too long we've been told about "us" and "them." Each and every election we see a new slate of arguments and ads telling us that "they" are the problem, not "us." But there can be no "them" in America. There's only us.

℘

Our Founders saw themselves in the light of posterity. We can do no less. Anyone who has ever watched a child's eyes wander into sleep knows what posterity is. Posterity is the world to come—the world for whom we hold our ideals, from whom we have borrowed our planet, and to whom we bear sacred responsibility.

* *

To renew America, we must meet challenges abroad as well as at home. There is no longer division between what is foreign and what is domestic—the world economy, the world environment, the world AIDS crisis, the world arms race—they affect us all.

☙

From this joyful mountaintop of celebration, we hear a call to service in the valley. We have heard the trumpets. We have changed the guard. And now, each in our way, and with God's help, we must answer the call.

☙

And what a century it has been. America became the world's mightiest industrial power; saved the world from tyranny in two world wars and a long cold war; and time and again, reached out across the globe to millions who, like us, longed for the blessings of liberty.

☙

The divide of race has been America's constant curse. And each new wave of immigrants gives new targets to old prejudices. Prejudice and contempt, cloaked in the pretense of religious or political conviction are no different. These forces have nearly destroyed our nation in the past. They plague us still. They fuel the fanaticism of terror. And they torment the lives of millions in fractured nations all around the world.

☙

Now, each of us must hold high the torch of citizenship in our own lives. None of us can finish the race alone. We can only achieve our destiny together— one hand, one generation, one American connecting to another.

Martin Luther King's dream was the American Dream. His quest is our quest: the ceaseless striving to live out our true creed. Our history has been built on such dreams and labors. And by our dreams and labors we will redeem the promise of America in the 21st century.

❧

And so, my fellow Americans, we must be strong, for there is much to dare. The demands of our time are great and they are different. Let us meet them with faith and courage, with patience and a grateful and happy heart. Let us shape the hope of this day into the noblest chapter in our history. Yes, let us build our bridge. A bridge wide enough and strong enough for every American to cross over to a blessed land of new promise.

❧

So look around here, look around here. Old or young, healthy as a horse or a person with a disability that hasn't kept you down, man or woman, Native American, native-born, immigrant, straight or gay— whatever—the test ought to be: I believe in the Constitution, the Bill of Rights and the Declaration of Independence. I believe in religious liberty, I believe in freedom of speech, and I believe in working hard and playing by the rules. I'm showing up for work tomorrow. I'm building that bridge to the 21st century.

❧

I am often troubled as I try hard here to create a new sense of common purpose . . . we oftentimes get so caught up in the babble of the moment, the heat of the moment . . . that sometimes we forget that we are all in this because we are seeking a good that helps all Americans.

> My fellow Americans, after these four, good, hard years, I still believe in a place called Hope, a place called America.

We will stand mighty for peace and freedom, and maintain a strong defense against terror and destruction. Our children will sleep free from the threat of nuclear, chemical or biological weapons.

✿

Modern science has confirmed what ancient faiths have always taught: the most important fact of life is our common humanity. Therefore, we should do more than just tolerate our diversity—we should honor it and celebrate it.

✿

If you go back to the beginning of this country, the great strength of America, as de Tocqueville pointed out when he came here a long time ago, has always been our ability to associate with people who were different from ourselves and to work together to find common ground. And in this day everybody has a responsibility to do more of that. We simply cannot wait for a tornado, a fire or a flood to behave like Americans ought to behave in dealing with one another.

* *

Building one America is our most important
mission—"the foundation for many generations," of
every other strength we must build for this new
century. Money cannot buy it. Power cannot compel it.
Technology cannot create it. It can only come from the
human spirit.

*

I ask you to join in a re-United States. We need to
empower our people so they can take more
responsibility for their own lives in a world that is ever
smaller, where everyone counts. We need a new spirit of
community, a sense that we are all in this together, or the
American Dream will continue to wither. Our destiny is
bound up with the destiny of every other American.

*

We must remember that America cannot lead in the
world unless here at home we weave the threads of our
coat of many colors into the fabric of one America. As
we become ever more diverse, we must work harder to
unite around our common values and our common
humanity. We must work harder to overcome our
differences, in our hearts and in our laws. We must
treat all our people with fairness and dignity, regardless
of their race, religion, gender or sexual orientation,
and regardless of when they arrived in our country;
always moving toward the more perfect union of our
founders' dreams.

GEORGE W. BUSH

43RD PRESIDENT • 2001–
Born: July 6, 1948, in New Haven, Connecticut

Wife: Laura Welch

Religion: Methodist

Education: Yale University, Harvard Business School

Other political offices: Governor of Texas

The son of the forty-first president, George W. Bush declared a war on terrorism following the September 11, 2001, attacks on the World Trade Center in New York and the Pentagon in Washington. Prior to becoming president, George W. Bush served as the governor of Texas and as the president of the Texas Rangers baseball team.

America is successful because of the hard work and creativity and enterprise of our people. These were the true strengths of our economy before September 11, and they are our strengths today.

☙

You can't put democracy and freedom back into a box.

☙

Unity . . . Resolve . . . Freedom. These are the hallmarks of the American spirit. Freedom and fear are now at war, and the strength of a nation relies on the resolve and determination of its people. Our nation— this generation—will lift a dark threat of violence for our people and our future. We will rally the world to this cause by our efforts, by our courage. We will not tire, we will not falter, and we will not fail.

☙

Americans are generous and strong and decent, not because we believe in ourselves, but because we hold beliefs beyond ourselves. When this spirit of citizenship is missing, no government program can replace it. When this spirit is present, no wrong can stand against it.

☙

I have faith that with God's help we as a nation will move forward together as one nation, indivisible. And together we will create an America that is open, so every citizen has access to the American dream; an America that is educated, so every child has the keys to realize that dream; and an America that is united in our diversity and our shared American values that are larger than race or party.

America is a nation full of good fortune, with so much to be grateful for. But we are not spared from suffering. In every generation, the world has produced enemies of human freedom. They have attacked America, because we are freedom's home and defender. And the commitment of our fathers is now the calling of our time.

ᴣ

We've defeated freedom's enemies before, and we will defeat them again. We have refused to live in a state of panic or in a state of denial. There is a difference between being alert and being intimidated and this great nation will never be intimidated.

ᴣ

Freedom and fear, justice and cruelty, have always been at war, and we know that God is not neutral between them.

ᴣ

I will not forget the wound to our country and those who inflicted it. I will not yield, I will not rest, I will not relent in waging this struggle for freedom and security for the American people.

ᴣ

As long as the United States of America is determined and strong, this will not be an age of terror. This will be an age of liberty here and across the world.

ᴣ

Freedom itself was attacked this morning by a faceless coward, and freedom will be defended.

This is not, however, just America's fight. And what is at stake is not just America's freedom. This is the world's fight. This is civilization's fight. This is the fight of all who believe in progress and pluralism, tolerance and freedom.

Encouraging responsibility is not a search for scapegoats; it is a call to conscience. And though it requires sacrifice, it brings a deeper fulfillment.

Tonight, we are a country awakened to danger and called to defend freedom. Our grief has turned to anger and anger to resolution. Whether we bring our enemies to justice or bring justice to our enemies, justice will be done.

✦

If our country does not lead the cause for freedom, it will not be led.

✦

Through much of the last century, America's faith in freedom and democracy was a rock in a raging sea. Now it is a seed upon the wind, taking root in many nations.

America, at its best, matches a commitment to principle with a concern for civility. A civil society demands from each of us good will and respect, fair dealing and forgiveness.

A

This is a day when all Americans from every walk of life unite in our resolve for justice and peace. . . . America has stood down enemies before, and we will do so this time.

A

Freedom and fear are at war. The advance of human freedom, the great achievement of our time and the great hope of every time, now depends on us.

A

A great people has been moved to defend a great nation. Terrorist attacks can shake the foundations of our biggest buildings, but they cannot touch the foundation of America. These acts shattered steel, but they cannot dent the steel of American resolve. America was targeted for attack because we're the brightest beacon for freedom and opportunity in the world. And no one will keep that light from shining. Today, our nation saw evil, the very worst of human nature. And we responded with the best of America— with the daring of our rescue workers, with the caring for strangers and neighbors who came to give blood and help in any way they could.

A

We will make no distinction between the terrorists who committed these acts and those who harbor them.

★ ★

It is the American story—a story of flawed and fallible people, united across the generations by grand and enduring ideals. The grandest of these ideals is an unfolding American promise that everyone belongs, that everyone deserves a chance—that no insignificant person was ever born.

ૐ

Sometimes in life we are called to do great things. But as a saint of our times has said, every day we are called to do small things with great love. The most important tasks of a democracy are done by everyone.

ૐ

The enemies of liberty and our country should make no mistake. America remains engaged in the world, by history and by choice, shaping a balance of power that favors freedom. We will defend our allies and our interests. We will show purpose without arrogance. We will meet aggression and bad faith with resolve and strength. And to all nations, we will speak for the values that gave our nation birth.

ૐ

Today we affirm a new commitment to live out our nation's promise through civility, courage, compassion and character.

ૐ

Use power to help people. For we are given power not to advance our own purposes nor to make a great show in the world, nor a name. There is but one just use of power and it is to serve people.

Index

Note: Index entries are key words or concepts within the quotations.

Index

Index